You Should See Us Now

A Play

Peter Tinniswood

Samuel French – London
New York – Sydney – Toronto – Hollywood

ISBN 0 573 11512 5

YOU SHOULD SEE US NOW

First presented at the Stephen Joseph Theatre In The Round, Scarborough, in 1981, with the following cast:

Graham Carey	Russell Dixon
Ernest Rowley	Graeme Eton
Pamela Rowley, his wife	Carole Boyd
Sheila Chilton, divorced from Graham	Lavinia Bertram
Mrs Mitten, her mother	Susan Vebel
Kate Cockburn	Christine Kavanagh

The Play directed by Alan Ayckbourn
Designed by Edward Lipscomb

Subsequently presented at Greenwich Theatre on 31st January, 1983, with the following cast:

Graham	Christopher Cazenove
Ernest	Simon Cadell
Pamela	Delia Lindsay
Sheila	Joanna van Gyseghem
Mrs Mitten	Pauline Yates
Kate	Francesca Gonshaw

The play directed by John Adams
Designed by Bernard Culshaw

The action takes place in Graham's house and garden
Time — the present

ACT I
SCENE 1   The drawing-room. Afternoon
SCENE 2   The garden. A few seconds later
SCENE 3   The drawing-room. A few seconds later
SCENE 4   The garden. An hour later
SCENE 5   The drawing-room. A few seconds later
SCENE 6   The children's bedroom. Half an hour later
SCENE 7   The drawing-room. Half an hour later

ACT II
SCENE 1   The garden. Mid-morning, the following day
SCENE 2   The drawing-room. A few seconds later
SCENE 3   The children's bedroom. A little later
SCENE 4   The drawing-room. Half an hour later
SCENE 5   The drawing-room. A few seconds later
SCENE 6   The drawing-room. A few seconds later
SCENE 7   The drawing-room. A few minutes later
SCENE 8   The garden. A few minutes later
SCENE 9   The drawing-room. A few seconds later
SCENE 10 The drawing-room. A few minutes later
SCENE 11 The drawing-room. A few minutes later
SCENE 12 The bedroom. A few minutes later
SCENE 13 The drawing-room. A few minutes later

You Should See Us Now was first presented at the Stephen Joseph Theatre In The Round, Scarborough, and it is on that production that this Acting Edition is based. The photograph on page vi is also from that production. However the play can easily be adapted for a proscenium stage.

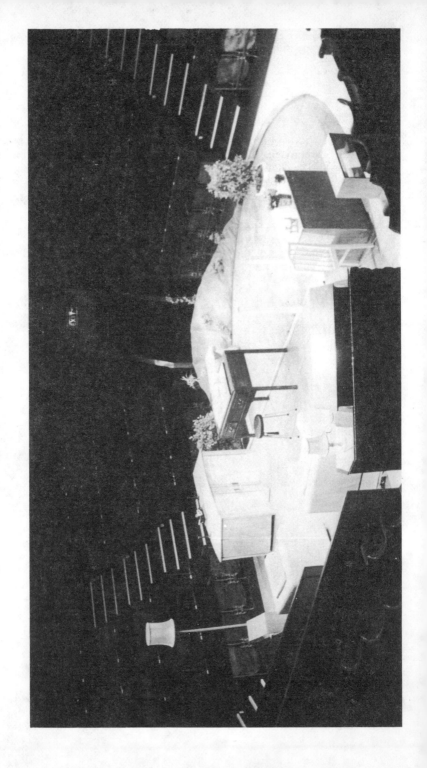

ACT I

Scene 1

The drawing-room of Graham Carey's house. Afternoon

There are french windows leading to the garden. It is spacious. Ernest Rowley is sitting at the table pretending he's driving a bus. He drum-drums with his voice and heaves his hands around as though he were steering the bus round a tight corner

Unseen by Ernest, Graham Carey enters with a tray on which is a bottle of wine and one glass

Graham stares at him silently for a moment. They are both aged around 40. Ernest, however, is on the plump side and looks older than his years. Graham is slim and wiry

Graham Ding ding. (*Louder*) I said — ding ding.

Ernest (*turning*) Oh hullo.

Graham Driving your bus again?

Ernest That's right.

Graham Like driving a bus, do you, Ernest?

Ernest Ra-ther. And it's so much easier these days since they've brought automatic gears in. Is that wine?

Graham Yes.

Ernest Excellento, old boy. Just what the doctor ordered.

Graham Now wait a minute, Ernest.

Ernest Yes?

Graham Do you really think it's wise to drink and drive?

Ernest (*slapping his thigh with pleasure*) Good one, Graham. Stinkeroo. Do you know, if there's one thing I like, it's a damn good joke. Particularly if it makes you laugh. Did you make it up yourself?

Graham All my own work, Ernest. (*He proceeds to make his way to the table with his tray and his wine, desperately trying to avoid the cat, which is twining itself round his legs. You can't see the cat, of course*) This blasted cat. Get out of the way. Why do cats always twine themselves round your legs like this? Why do they always wait for you to put your foot down and then dart right underneath it and . . . Get out of the way. (*He crashes the tray on to the table and begins to chase the cat*) Come here. Come here, you little swine. Come here, you monster. (*He corners it under the dresser*) Got you. Cornered. (*He squats down*) OK, buster, come on out with your hands up. The game's up. It's a fair cop. Don't you spit at me, sunshine. Don't you raise your claws at me. (*He begins to scrabble for it under the dresser*) Come out of that. Listen. I intend to be master in my own house. Do you understand that? Has it

sunk into your thick square head? I *will* be master in my own house and . . .
Ouch. You swine. You devil. (*He makes a grab for it and emerges triumphantly holding it by the scruff of the neck at arm's length and taking it to the french windows*) You see, you don't like that, do you? It's undignified, isn't it? It offends you, doesn't it? Well, listen to me, sunshine, it offends me when you trip me on the stairs, when you dig up my plants in the garden, when you sleep on the clean sheets in the airing cupboard, when you . . . I won't have it. Do you understand? I *will* be master in my own house. (*He opens the french windows and hurls the cat out*) Get out. And stay out. (*He closes the windows and turns to Ernest with a smile of triumph*)

Ernest I want to go home.

Graham You've only just come.

Ernest I know.

Graham Then why do you want to go home?

Ernest I miss our toilet.

Graham What?

Ernest Oh, it's no reflection on yours, old boy.

Graham Thank you.

Ernest No, as a matter of fact, I think your toilet's right out of the top drawer, old boy. Gives you a real welcome when you go in. Makes you feel at ease. It's just that . . . Well, it's just that I can't cope with other people's ablution procedures.

Graham What? (*He begins to pour himself a glass of wine*)

Ernest Take this morning for example. I heard you go in. I heard you go out. I heard Pamela go in. I heard Pamela go out. And then someone else went in.

Graham But there's no-one else in the house, Ernest.

Ernest Precisely. I waited half an hour in absolute agony. Sheer torture, old boy. Came out in a sweat. Desperate measures needed. So I dashed to the toilet, kicked open the door and do you know what?

Graham What?

Ernest It was the cat. It was the cat I heard go in. It was lying in the bath fast asleep.

Graham I'll kill it. I swear to God I'll kill it.

Ernest No need to do that. Just let me go home.

Graham That, Ernest, is a matter for Pamela. If you want to go home, if you want to desert your closest friend in the hour of his direst need, so be it. But sort it out with Pamela.

Ernest Difficult.

Graham I know.

Ernest I don't think you do.

Graham Why?

Ernest Well . . . Well, have you noticed anything peculiar between me and Pamela since we've been here?

Graham Yes. Yes, I have, Ernest. You sleep in separate bedrooms, don't you? And she's very rude to you. Hectoring, patronizing, contemptuous——

Ernest Oh, I don't mean that. I mean something *really* peculiar. A change in our attitudes to each other. A basic and fundamental change in our relationship.

Graham That, Ernest, I have not noticed.

Ernest Good. That means it doesn't show.

Graham What doesn't show?

Ernest That I've fallen in love.

Graham What?

Ernest I've fallen in love. With another woman.

Graham Which other woman?

Ernest My dentist.

Graham I think I'll go in the garden and mither the cat.

Ernest What a woman, Graham. So gentle. So tender. So adept.

Graham Good God. You've been to bed with her?

Ernest No, no. I'm talking about her qualities as a dentist.

Graham I see, Ernest.

Ernest Do you know, Graham, I had three fillings last week and I didn't feel a thing. Not a thing. So gentle. So tender. So adept.

Graham How advanced are you in your relationship with your dentist?

Ernest Well, I've had six appointments so far. And I've got another two next week.

Graham I don't mean that. I mean, how often have you taken her out? Have you wined her and dined her? Have you had secret assignations in art galleries and railway waiting-rooms? Have you rented a flat in Maida Vale and taken her to bed and——

Ernest Good Lord, no. A chap doesn't do things like that with his dentist. A chap could get struck off her list. And then where would I be? Half-way through my treatment and——

Graham What have you done with her then?

Ernest Nothing.

Graham Nothing?

Ernest Nothing except fall madly head over heels in love with her.

Graham Poor old you.

Ernest Yes. Poor old me. I say, old boy.

Graham Yes?

Ernest Do you think I might have a drop of that wine?

Graham Of course, Ernest. Sorry. How rude of me. (*He begins to pour a glass of wine then notices something outside the french windows*) That cat's chasing the birds again. (*He races to the windows and hammers on them*) Get out of it. Get away. Clear off.

He turns and gulps down the wine, much to Ernest's disappointment

I hate cats, Ernest. I loathe them. I despise them. Do you know, Ernest, when Sheila walked out, she took every single one of her possessions. Everything. Except the cat. Why? Why, Ernest? Why? Was it some fiendish plot? Is she encapsulated deep in the soul of that cat? That's it. She is. That cat is Sheila with a skin on. And she's spying on me. Tormenting me, torturing me . . . Sorry. Sorry, Ernest. You were saying?

Ernest I was asking for a drop of wine.

Graham Course you were. Sorry. (*He begins to pour another glass*)

Ernest And I was talking about my dentist.

Graham Ah yes. And do you recommend her?

Ernest Ra-ther. As dentists go, she's absolutely A1. Excellento.

Graham Good. Jolly good. (*He pours out the glass of wine and drinks it himself*)

Ernest looks bitterly disappointed

Ernest It's my time of life, you know.

Graham What is?

Ernest This affair.

Graham What affair?

Ernest With my dentist, old boy. I wish you'd pay attention.

Graham Sorry.

Ernest There are others, you know.

Graham Really? How fascinating. How intriguing. How fantastically, amazingly——

Ernest You don't have to pay all that much attention.

Graham Sorry.

Ernest All I'm saying is I have got other affairs. I mean, I've got this most fearful crush on the lady in the dog-biscuit shop.

Graham Good for you.

Ernest It's not that she's beautiful. Well, I suppose she could be—in context. It's just that ... Well, do you know what I'm trying to get at, Graham?

Graham Not entirely, Ernest.

Ernest I need to be unfaithful. I need to have an affair, Graham. A real affair with kissing and grunting and sharp toenails. Good Lord above, you've had enough in your time. I mean to say, old boy, it's all those affairs which have got you into the mess you're in now.

Graham Thank you very much.

Ernest Not at all.

Graham So what are you saying?

Ernest I'm saying I want my life to be in a mess. I want my life to be totally chaotic. I want danger, Graham. I want romance and passion and all that sort of rot. Do you know, I've always fancied having an affair with an older woman.

Graham Now that is very good thinking, Ernest.

Ernest An older woman. Mature. Experienced. Smokes Turkish cigarettes. The trouble is all the older women I fancy are younger than me.

Graham Have a glass of wine.

Ernest Thank you very much.

Graham begins to pour another glass of wine

You see, Graham, I've reached that time in life when a chap starts asking himself fundamental questions.

Graham What fundamental questions, Ernest?

Ernest You know, old boy. What is the meaning of life? What is reality? Who thought up those names they put on the sides of goods wagons.

Graham What? What are you talking about?

Ernest You know. Goods wagons. On the railways. They have names on the sides. Sea cow, shark, whale, mermaid, sturgeon — things like that. I think the chappie who thought up those names was a genius. One of the great giants of English literature.

Graham You're being silly.

Ernest I know. It's the only way to cope.

Graham That's acting like a child. (*He gulps down his glass of wine*)

Ernest I know. The only time I could ever cope with life was when I was a child. I was good at sums then. People respected me for it. I'm still good at sums. But what respect do I get now? Pamela treats me with contempt. The lady from the dog-biscuit shop totally ignores me. Do you know, old boy, when I was a child, I could take a privet leaf, fold it carefully, dampen it with the tip of my tongue and blow it like a mouth organ and play a tune. Really. I could. And I got respect. I got respect for being clumsy. People pay attention to clumsy people. I was a fool, too. I was fat. I was frightened of cricket balls. People pay attention to people who are frightened of cricket balls. It's one of the laws of nature.

Graham (*laughing*) Yes.

Ernest I haven't changed from those days, Graham. I'm still the same. I'm still frightened of cricket balls. I can still play tunes on a privet leaf. I'm still me. And what happens? People ignore me and treat me with contempt. I wish I were a little boy again. (*He half-heartedly begins to drive his bus again*)

Graham (*softly*) Have a glass of wine.

Ernest I thought you'd never offer, old boy.

Graham pours a glass of wine. Ernest looks at it longingly, licking his lips with anticipation

Graham There you are.

He hands him the glass. Ernest is just about to drink it

At that moment, Pamela enters, marches across to him and snatches it from his hand. Pamela is in her mid-thirties. She's brisk and efficient

Pamela Thank you, Ernest. We don't drink wine at this time of the day, do we?

Ernest I haven't been drinking wine, Pamela. He has.

Pamela And we don't snitch on our friends either, do we? Now then, Graham, it's all arranged.

Graham What's all arranged?

Pamela The party.

Graham What party?

Pamela The children's party.

Graham I don't follow you, Pamela.

Pamela It's simple enough, Graham. I have arranged a party for your children.

Ernest Oh Lord. I want to go home.

Pamela I'll ignore that remark, Ernest.

Ernest You see, Graham, you see. What did I tell you? People ignore me.

Graham What's all this about parties, Pamela?

Pamela There's no need to sound so dismissive, Graham. It might interest you to know that I have spent the last two hours visiting your neighbours with the purpose of inviting their children to a party at your home.

Graham But I don't like parties.

Pamela It is not for you, Graham. It is for your children.

Graham I don't like children either.

Pamela You should have thought of that before you started breeding.

Ernest I say, Pamela. Steady on.

Pamela Don't you look at me in that tone of voice, Ernest. You're on a very sticky wicket when it comes to that subject.

Ernest What subject?

Pamela Hanky-panky.

Ernest Hanky-panky?

Pamela Don't shout.

Ernest (*softly*) Hanky-panky?

Pamela Let's drop the subject, shall we, Ernest? Enough. I don't wish to speak any further about it. As far as I am concerned it is now a closed book.

Ernest It always was with you.

Pamela What?

Ernest Hanky-panky.

Pamela Ernest.

Ernest Yes, Pamela?

Pamela When we are told to drop a subject, what do we do?

Ernest We drop it.

Pamela Precisely. And stop lounging like that in your chair. Sit up, pull your shoulders back and stop fiddling with your buttons.

Graham I don't want a party.

Pamela Graham Carey.

Graham Yes, Pamela?

Pamela You are having a party.

Graham Yes, Pamela.

Pamela You have asked me here to help out with your children. Am I right?

Graham Yes, Pamela. You're right.

Pamela Well then, leave it all to me, shall we? You see, Graham, the secret of having children to stay is to keep them constantly occupied. Don't let them settle for a minute. Harry them from pillar to post. Pester them. Badger them. Keep them constantly on the move. The golden rule with children is this—if in doubt, thwack them.

Ernest You make them sound like criminals.

Pamela Precisely, Ernest. That is just the way to treat them. Like criminals children are deeply anti-social elements in the community. They're disruptive. They're destructive. They're totally selfish and utterly lacking in a sense of common decency.

Graham Then why give them a party?

Pamela For precisely the reason that the police tolerate the existence of illegal drinking clubs.

Ernest Beg pardon?

Pamela The police tolerate illegal drinking clubs, Ernest, because they know that is where the criminals will congregate. Therefore they know where to find them. It's the same with children's parties. They're all together under one roof. Therefore you know where to find them. They are very easily thwackable.

Ernest I want to go home.

Pamela No, you don't, Ernest. And let me explain why. We are friends of Graham. And Graham is in need. And when friends are in need, we rally round, don't we?

Ernest Yes, but——

Pamela Never mind "Yes, but", Ernest. Think of your responsibilities.

Ernest What responsibilities?

Pamela Your responsibilities. Your responsibilities to Graham.

Ernest I keep telling you – I'm not responsible enough to have responsibilities.

Pamela Look at him, Graham. Take a long hard look at him. Have you ever in the whole of your life seen such a pathetic creature?

Graham He's all right.

Pamela What?

Graham (*sharply*) He's all right, Pamela. He's fine. He's my friend.

Pamela Your friend, eh? Well, do you know what your friend did, when I told him we were coming here to stay with you?

Graham I'm not interested, Pamela.

Pamela Oh yes you are. You've got to learn, Graham, that in this world no-one is to be trusted. No-one. This is a big cruel world, Graham. You're on your own. Friends are all very well. But deep inside the heart of every friend there's traitor screaming to get out and do you harm.

Ernest I say, Pamela. Steady on.

Pamela Steady on? Look at you. Graham's friend, eh? Well, what was your attitude when I told you we were coming to stay with him? Excuses. Sulks. Nose-bleeds. Constipation. And don't tell me you didn't cut your thumb on purpose on that tin of corned beef.

Ernest I'm clumsy, Pamela. I'm congenitally clumsy.

Pamela Excuses, Ernest. Excuses, excuses. (*She mimics him*) "Don't make me go, Pamela." "I'm allergic to cats." "I can't work the toilet lights." "I've got an appointment with the dentist."

Ernest (*alarmed*) Beg pardon?

Pamela Excuses, Ernest. Excuses, Graham. The worm turns. The friend is shown up in his true colours.

Graham I happen to like them.

Pamela What?

Graham Ernest's true colours.

Pamela Nonsense.

Graham It is not nonsense. Before you came in, we were talking, Ernest and I. We were talking intimately. Confidentially.

Ernest I say, old boy. Steady on. Remember the old fillings.

Graham We were talking and it was all very interesting.

Pamela Yes, I'm sure it was, Graham. And what was the subject of your talk? Barmaids? Football? Dirty jokes?

Graham We were talking about cats.

Pamela Cats?

Graham I wish I were a cat.

Ernest Beg pardon?

Graham I admire cats. All slinky they are. All sly and evil. Lissom. Know what I mean, Ernest?

Ernest Ra-ther. They're lissom all right. The way they can lick their whatsits without——

Graham Miaow. Yaark, yaark. (*He crouches on all fours*)

Pamela What on earth are you doing?

Graham I'm a cat, Pamela. I'm showing you I love you. (*He begins to wind himself round her legs*)

Pamela For heaven's sake, Graham.

Graham Miaow. Yaark. Yaark, Pamela. Yaark.

Pamela (*pushing him away*) Graham.

Graham Yes, Pamela?

Pamela On your feet.

Graham Yes, Pamela. (*He gets up*)

Pamela There is work to be done, Graham. Sheila and your children are due here in fifteen minutes' time. Now have you got everything prepared?

Graham Yes, Pamela. I've locked the booze away. I've put all my books in the loft. I've battened down the study.

Ernest We've informed the police.

Graham And the fire brigade.

Ernest And the civil defence. And the——

Pamela (*fiercely*) Men! Men!

They fall silent

Men! You're worse than children.

She storms out

There is silence for a moment

Ernest What's your favourite food, old boy?

Graham My favourite, favourite food?

Ernest Yes. Your favourite, favourite food.

Graham Beefburger and chips.

Ernest Mine, too. And who's your favourite cricketer?

Graham Of all time?

Ernest Of all time.

Graham Bob Appleyard.

Ernest Mine, too, old boy. Mine, too. There's friendship for you.

Graham Yes, Ernest, there's friendship.

They embrace warmly

Shall we go out in the garden?
Ernest Why not, old boy? And I'll tell you what.
Graham What?
Ernest I'll find a privet leaf, and I'll play you a tune.

They exit through the french windows into the garden, Graham taking the bottle of wine and glass with him

Scene 2

The garden. A few seconds later

Graham and Ernest enter from the french windows, Graham carrying the glass and bottle of wine

Ernest Can she see us?
Graham Not if we stand here.
Ernest Excellento. I'll have that glass of wine.
Graham Of course. Right away.

Ernest watches Graham pouring the wine with slavering lips

Ernest Thought we'd never get round to this. Sheer torture, old boy. Watching you guzzling back the old vino—excruciating. And then just as I'm about to have my snorter at long last Pamela walks in and——

Graham moves to hand him the glass

I say, thanks a million, old boy.

Before Graham hands over the glass he sees the cat

Graham That cat. That bloody cat's digging up my delphiniums. Get out of it. (*He hurls the wine bottle at the cat and then charges at the shrubbery, still holding the glass of wine*) Get out of it. Clear off. (*He turns and walks back to Ernest*) Sorry about that, Ernest. Here's your wine.

He hands him the glass. Ernest looks at it

Ernest It's empty. You spilled it chasing the cat.
Graham Blast. I'm sorry, Ernest. Wait there and I'll—— Blast.
Ernest What's the matter?
Graham I've locked all the hooch away.
Ernest No matter. I'm used to it. I'm that sort of person.
Graham I've got to lock it away. Last time the kids came to stay Crispin got into the drinks cupboard and drank half a bottle of egg flip.
Ernest Egg flip. I say. Yerrrk! Why didn't he go for the malt whisky?
Graham He's only eight.
Ernest I wish I were eight.
Graham Poor old Ernest.
Ernest I had a green fairy cycle when I was eight. Fairy cycle. Why did they

call them fairy cycles? Curious. My fairy cycle was bottle green and it had black mudguards. They always used to clank. I'm that sort of person.

As he's talking Graham wanders over to a privet bush and carefully selects a leaf

When I was eight I saw Dwight D. Eisenhower. Not *the* Dwight D. Eisenhower. Dwight D. Eisenhower, the locomotive. It was standing in Darlington Station. So were we. That's why we saw it. Beautiful thing. Steam snorting out of its cylinders. Flanks quivering. The engine-driver was eating egg sandwiches. I wish I'd been an engine-driver.

Graham (*handing him the leaf*) Here you are.

Ernest What is it?

Graham A privet leaf.

Ernest I say, old boy.

Graham Do you want to play me a tune?

Ernest Ra-ther. By jove, this takes me back. Excellento, old boy. (*He begins to fold the leaf carefully*) Very tricky operation this, you know.

Graham I'm sure.

Ernest Fold it very carefully. See? Don't crack it. Very very careful. See?

Graham I'm very impressed, Ernest.

Ernest And now dampen it ever so slightly with the tongue. See?

Graham Terrific.

Ernest And now we're all ready. So what would you like me to play, old boy?

Graham I leave it entirely to you, Ernest.

Ernest No, no. It's your choice. I'm your guest. It's only polite that you should choose the tune.

Graham I honestly don't mind, Ernest.

Ernest No, no, I insist.

Graham Well, what if I chose a tune you can't play?

Ernest Now steady on, old boy. Are you inferring that I can't——

Graham I'm not inferring anything, Ernest. It's your privet leaf. You've prepared it. Now carry it through to the bitter end and play the tune you want to play.

Ernest Shan't.

Graham What?

Ernest It's not fair.

Graham Ernest, I don't quite follow.

Ernest I want to go home.

Graham Oh, Ernest. Ernest, Ernest, Ernest. (*He hugs him warmly*) Poor old Ernest.

Ernest You are my best friend, aren't you?

Graham Of course I am.

Ernest Really my best friend?

Graham Sure. Really your best friend.

Ernest My really, really best friend?

Pause. Graham looks at him with compassion

Graham I miss you, Ernest.

Ernest I miss you, too, old boy. I curse to the innermost cockles of my heart the day Pamela insisted on moving away from here.

Graham I know you do.

Ernest Suburbia! I loved suburbia. Look at it. Dull, boring, predictable. Just like me.

Graham Just like you, Ernest.

Ernest I used to love that walk home from the station in the evening. Friendly concrete lamp posts. Pollarded trees. Cars gleaming in the driveways. Television sets flickering. Steel tips clacking away on the pavement. So comforting. So reassuring.

Graham Sure, Ernest. Sure.

Ernest When I was eight, I used to sit by the window in my bedroom waiting for Father to come home in the evening. It was his brolly I used to hear first. Very distinctive. It always had a loose ferrule on its tip. Ferrule? What a lovely word. Ferrule. I had a bay window in my bedroom, and, if I craned my neck and pressed my nose against the glass, I could see him as he crossed the road. Always the same place. The snicket that ran between the cedar garage with the tarpaulin roof and that funny little sub power station with the flash of lightning painted on the door. Always the same place. And he'd stop in the middle of the road, and he'd sniff the air, and he'd breathe in deeply, and he'd smile and nod his head. He looked really happy. Contented. And there'd be a bounce to his heels as he walked down the front drive. And I'd run downstairs to meet him. And he'd pat me on the head, and he'd say: "Hullo, old boy." Always the same. Comforting. Reassuring. And then one evening he didn't come home.

Graham No?

Ernest No. He'd run off with the lady from the cake shop.

Graham Poor old Ernest.

Ernest I loved it here. Suburbia. Perfection.

Graham You don't like the country?

Ernest Hate it, old boy. Loathe it. It's so squelchy.

Graham What?

Ernest And that village pub. I loathe it.

Graham Why?

Ernest It's so warm, so friendly, so welcoming.

Graham And what's wrong with that?

Ernest It's the responsibility I feel for it. The landlord makes you feel that he's running the pub for you personally. No-one else. And if you don't go in every night, he'd commit suicide or something. So into the pub I go every night. And I don't like beer. It's so squelchy. It wouldn't be so bad if they served Tizer. Tizer. I used to drink gallons of Tizer when I was eight. So much better than Vimto, old boy.

Graham (*after a pause*) Are you managing all right?

Ernest So far. We're still living off the proceeds of the old golden handshake.

Graham Ah.

Ernest I was a fool, you know, Graham.

Graham In what way?

Ernest I should have gone into a secure job. You see, old boy, as soon as there's a slump or a recession double glazing goes out of the window.

Graham So what sort of business should you have gone into?

Ernest Water biscuits.

Graham What?

Ernest Well, think about it, old boy. You never read of a slump in the water-biscuit industry, do you? You never read headlines: "Water-biscuit closures — millions made redundant". You see, old boy, whatever the state of the nation, people still want water biscuits.

Graham I suppose they do.

Ernest And raffle tickets.

Graham What?

Ernest Raffle tickets. People always want raffle tickets. That's what I should have been in—raffle tickets. Could have branched out into cloakroom tickets and—— I say.

Graham Yes?

Ernest I think the cat's doing something rather disgusting in your michaelmas daisies.

Graham (*racing to the shrubbery*) I'll kill it. I swear to God I'll kill it. Get out of it. Clear off, you little square-headed swine.

Pamela enters

Pamela They're just coming down the road.

Graham What?

Pamela Your brood are here. The car's turning into the drive now.

Ernest Oh, Lord. Well, I'd better be——

Pamela You certainly had, Ernest. What do we do when guests arrive in the house? We go into the kitchen and wash our hands, don't we?

Ernest Yes, Pamela. Wash our hands. That's right. (*He begins to move towards the kitchen*) Well then, old boy. Lots of luck, eh? Chin up and . . . and . . .

Pamela And we don't dither and waffle either. We do it straight away, don't we?

Ernest Straight away. Yes. Straight away.

Ernest exits to the kitchen

Pamela pauses for a moment and then walks to Graham

Pamela (*tenderly*) Nervous?

Graham A bit.

Pamela You're bound to be.

Graham I suppose so.

Pamela Don't let her intimidate you.

Graham No.

Pamela Stand up to her. Be firm.

Graham Yes. Of course.

Pamela (*moving very close to him*) I won't let her harm you, Graham. Pamela won't let her harm you.

She kisses him quite passionately. He stands stock still

There now. That was nice, wasn't it?

Graham nods. She takes him by the hand tenderly and leads him slowly to the drawing-room

Come on, Graham. Into the drawing-room you go. Compose yourself. Be calm. I'll let her in. But I won't let her harm you. Oh no. Pamela won't let her harm Graham. (*She pauses. Then briskly and efficiently*) Right then. In you go. Chop chop.

Graham exits through the french windows into the drawing-room

SCENE 3

The drawing-room. A few seconds later

Graham enters through the french windows from the garden

At the same time, Ernest enters through the hall door

Ernest She's just coming through the front door, old boy. She's brought her mother. Oh crumbs. Oh Lord. (*He rushes around*)
Graham Ernest.
Ernest Yes, old boy?
Graham What are you doing?
Ernest Looking for my ... Ah. It's here. My pocket compass.
Graham What?
Ernest My pocket compass, old boy. Never go anywhere without it. Except when I lose it, of course and then ... They're here. Good luck, old boy. Good luck.

Ernest dashes out through the french windows

Pamela enters through the hall door. She stands still and announces the guests like a master of ceremonies

Pamela Your ex-wife. Your ex-mother-in-law. And your ex-children.

Sheila and her mother, Mrs Mitten, enter. Sheila is elegant and beautiful and in her mid-thirties. Mrs Mitten is over-dressed with a strong Northern accent which obviously offends her daughter. Sheila turns and talks to the children who are still in the hall

Sheila No, not in here, children. You go and play in the garden. Daddy and I have something to discuss. When we've finished, you can come in and pay your respects to him. And remember—no throwing stones at the cat. Thank you. And thank you, Pamela. That will be all.
Pamela (*very sweetly, but fighting to keep cool*) Only too happy to oblige, Sheila. If you should want me, I shall be in the garden. Most likely throwing stones. At the cat. Most therapeutic. Good-day to you.

Pamela exits through the french windows

Mrs Mitten What's Lady Muck doing here?

Graham Pamela and Ernest are staying here to help out.

Sheila Help out?

Graham With the children.

Sheila I don't follow.

Graham It's perfectly easy. I'm here on my own, so I need help with the kids.

Sheila On your own?

Graham Yes.

Sheila So what's happened to Amelia?

Graham Well, she——

Sheila No. Wait a minute. Amelia was the one before, wasn't she? The one that came after her was . . . was . . . Help me, Graham. Come on, help me.

Graham Kate.

Sheila Kate. That's the one. So what's happened to Kate then?

Graham Yes . . . well . . . Well, the thing is . . . The thing is we've parted.

Mrs Mitten There you are. What did I tell you? He's a different woman in the house every time we come. This is no fit place to bring up children, isn't this, you know. It's like the Arabian Nights, is this.

Sheila Mother!

Mrs Mitten Don't you "Mother" me. As I say, I was brought up in a hard school. None of these flimmeries and fineries when I was a young lass. But my mother brought me up to lead a decent life with decent values and decent underclothes. And that's what I did to you. You always had satsumas at Christmas. There was always a box at the panto. When you was little you met Nat Jackley three times. In person, too. Nothing was too——

Sheila Mother!

Mrs Mitten And then you go and marry him and all that goes for nothing. I remember the first time you brought him home. He looked like a French onion-seller.

Graham Thank you.

Mrs Mitten You're welcome.

Graham Would you care for a drink?

Mrs Mitten You see, Sheila, you see. Booze-mad. We're not in the house five minutes and he's wanting to get us drunk.

Sheila He's being hospitable, Mother.

Mrs Mitten Hospitable! As I say, I was hospitable to him the first time he come to our house, and look what happens? He gets you pregnant twice and then he runs off with that cook from the school canteen.

Graham I did not run off with a cook from the school canteen. It was your daughter who walked out on me. It was your daughter who walked out of this house and left me . . .

Mrs Mitten Don't haggle. The end result was the same whatever happened. She was broken-hearted. You was gallivanting. And your children turned into chronic bed-wetters. As I say, you always was a wrong 'un.

Graham Thank you.

Mrs Mitten You're welcome. A modeller! What sort of job is that for a grown man?

Graham A very good job as a matter of fact. I earn a very good living out of it.

Sheila What are you doing now?

Graham "Prince Albert."

Sheila What?

Graham It's a Great Western locomotive. It's a commission for a museum in Stuttgart.

Mrs Mitten I didn't know they had museums in Stuttgart.

Graham There's a lot you don't know, Mrs Mitten.

Mrs Mitten Maybe. But there's one thing I do know—this is not a fit and proper place for my grandchildren to stay in. If I had my way, they'd not be allowed to come here at all.

Graham But on this matter, Mrs Mitten, you have not got your way. The access agreement states quite categorically that I am entitled to have my children during their school holidays and at other times arranged at mutual convenience. It does not say where I should have them. It does not say who should be here when I have them. If I wanted to, Mrs Mitten, I could have my children staying with me on the first floor of a French brothel with——

Mrs Mitten You see, you see. Sex-mad. As I say, Sheila, if you had any gumption about you, you'd pack those children in the automatic Volvo here and now, take them home and let him fight it out in the courts.

Graham You've got a Volvo, have you?

Sheila Yes.

Graham What happened to the BMW?

Mrs Mitten Don't tell him. It's personal, is that. All he's doing is fishing, so he'll have an excuse to dock the children's maintenance.

Sheila Mother, will you stop interfering.

Mrs Mitten Oh, I see. I see. Interfering, is it? Well, as I say, Sheila, you wasn't backwards in coming forwards for my help when meladdo here left you in the lurch with two small children and an ocelot fur coat that wasn't paid for.

Graham I did not leave your daughter in the lurch.

Mrs Mitten Don't haggle.

Sheila He's not haggling.

Mrs Mitten Hey up, hey up. Don't you interfere with me, young lady, when I'm having an argy bargy with him. That was your trouble all along. If you'd let me interfere with him the first time he come to our house with his dirty hankie and his dry-cleaner's tabs showing, none of this would ever have happened. As I say, Sheila, you could have had your choice of umpteen chartered accountants, when you was available.

Sheila Of course, Mother, of course. How foolish I was. How reckless. There was Geoffrey Singleton just waiting to be plucked from——

Mrs Mitten Geoffrey Singleton. Exactly. He might have big ears and buck teeth, but look what he's made of his life. He goes on an annual cruise on the *QE2*. Each year, too. And he's got a holiday cottage in North Wales.

Sheila It's just been burned down by the Welsh Nationalists.

Mrs Mitten Well, don't blame me for that. I never did like the Welsh any

road. All those male voice choirs and Maudie Edwards on the wireless—
there's something suspicious about a race what does that.

Graham How is Geoffrey Singleton by the way?

Sheila His wife's just run off with the local golf professional.

Mrs Mitten Golf! What a waste of time. Grown men getting into a tizz-wazz
about hitting a little white ball into a hole in the ground. Disgusting.
(*Pointing her finger at Graham*) Grown men spending all their time making
model railway engines. What next?

Graham What next, Mrs Mitten? What next? Well, I had thought of making
a model guillotine. Or maybe a model gas chamber. Or maybe a model
rack. You know what a rack is, Mrs Mitten? It's an object of torture.

Mrs Mitten Yes, and you're an object of torture to me. As I say, you looked
like a French onion-seller that first time you——

Sheila Mother! For heaven's sake will you give it a rest?

Mrs Mitten I see, I see. As I say, I know when I'm not wanted. Right then, get
on with it without me. I'm going upstairs to inspect his airing cupboard.
Now don't look at me like that. I was brought up in a hard school. And the
one thing I learned from having an outside petty with warped doors was
this—always maintain your airing cupboard proper. When I was a young
lass there was hundreds and thousands succumbed to TB because they
didn't air their clothes correctly. Well, I'm not having my grandchildren
going to bed in damp pyjamas. Now then, Sheila, do what business you've
got to do with him as quick as you can and then we'll be off and away in the
automatic Volvo.

Sheila Yes, Mother. Yes.

Mrs Mitten If I had my way——

Sheila (*very firmly leading her to the door*) Yes, Mother. Yes.

Mrs Mitten (*pausing at the door*) And I'll bet you anything he's not boiled his
flannels since the last time we was here.

Mrs Mitten slams the door as she exits

Sheila turns to Graham

Sheila Well then?

Graham Well then.

Pause

Would you care for a drink?

Sheila What happened to Kate?

Graham Ah, Kate. It's a very long and complicated story.

Sheila I'd like to hear it.

Graham I don't really see what it's got to do with you, Sheila.

Sheila (*very firmly*) I want to hear it.

Graham OK. Kate's an archivist, and we met at the——

Ernest enters through the french windows

Ernest Sorry to butt in, old boy, but . . . Oh, hullo, Sheila.

Sheila Hullo, Ernest.

Ernest Thank you.

Sheila Pardon?

Ernest I'm saying thank you for you saying hullo to me. Much appreciated. Thank you.

Sheila And how are you liking the country, Ernest?

Ernest Oh, it's absolutely frightful, old boy.

Sheila Really?

Ernest Ra-ther. Total absence of Tizer. Cows everywhere you look. And I keep getting these spots on my bum. Think it could be a shaving rash, but——

Graham Ernest.

Ernest Yes, old boy?

Graham What do you want?

Ernest Ah yes. It's your children.

Graham My children?

Ernest Well, Sheila's children as well. I mean, after all they were a joint project, weren't they?

Sheila What about the children, Ernest?

Ernest They say they're bored.

Graham Bored?

Ernest Yes. Well, I don't blame them. Quite frankly, old boy, so am I.

Graham Why don't you play cricket with them?

Ernest Cricket. I say, what a good idea. Excellento. Bags I bat first. Well then, Sheila, nice to have met you again. (*He shakes hands with her*)

Sheila Nice to have met you, too, Ernest.

Ernest Good. Jolly good. You're looking in damn good nick, Sheila. Keep it up. Yes. Well . . . (*He backs towards the french windows*)

Graham And don't hit the ball in the rose beds.

Ernest No. No, of course not. Tell you what, anyone who hits the ball in the rose bed is out. How about that?

Graham Very good, Ernest. Now will you kindly leave us.

Ernest Of course, old boy. Of course. Well, goodbye then, Sheila. My compliments on your togs. A1. Absolutely tip-top. Yes. Yes. Excellento.

Ernest exits through the french windows

Sheila You were saying?

Graham How's Bruce?

Sheila Bruce is blooming. You were saying about Kate.

Graham Ah. So I was. Well, Kate's an archivist and . . . Do the children get on with him?

Sheila Bruce?

Graham Yes.

Sheila The children adore Bruce. They worship him. So Kate's an archivist and you met her where?

Graham I met her in the——

Pamela enters through the hall door

Pamela I've just had occasion to have words with your mother, Sheila.

Sheila Really, Pamela?

Pamela Yes, Sheila. I caught her in the children's bedroom putting a mirror between the sheets.

Sheila That's to see if they've been aired properly.

Pamela I am well aware of that, Sheila. But we don't happen to be living in a terraced back-to-back in the depths of Salford.

Sheila Really, Pamela?

Pamela We happen to be living in a very desirable detached house in a very desirable part of a very desirable town. Here things do not get damp.

Sheila Don't they, Pamela? Well, what about Ernest?

Pamela I beg your pardon?

Graham Now come off it, you two. No squabbling, please. Please. I couldn't stand it. Give it a rest.

Pamela No, Graham, no. I will not give it a rest. What precisely do you mean, Sheila, when you say: "What about Ernest?"

Sheila Very simple, Pamela. You said things in this very desirable part of town do not get damp. Right?

Pamela Right.

Sheila Well, what about Ernest? He's more than damp. He's positively wringing wet.

Graham Now come off it, Sheila, there's no need to——

Pamela Shut up. Right. Right then. I've kept my mouth shut this past two years. Not a word have I said against you to Graham. I've tried to be strictly impartial. Well, no more. Finished. Let me tell you, Sheila Chilton, or whatever you call yourself now, I think you are without exception the——

Mrs Mitten enters from the hall brandishing a facecloth

Mrs Mitten What's this then? Go on—what is it? What is it? I'll tell you. It's a flannel. Just look at it. It's an absolute disgrace, is this flannel. As I say, I might have been brought up in a hard school, but my mother would turn over in her grave like a row of catherine wheels if she could see the state of this flannel.

Pamela Give it to me.

Mrs Mitten I most certainly will not. I'm taking this back in the automatic Volvo and I intend to present it as evidence.

Graham Evidence?

Mrs Mitten Evidence of your unsuitability to look after my grandchildren.

Pamela Give me that facecloth.

Pamela advances on her. Sheila rushes across

Sheila Don't you dare lay your hands on my mother.

Pamela Well, tell her to give me that facecloth.

Mrs Mitten It's not a facecloth. It's a flannel.

Pamela It's a facecloth. And it happens to be mine.

Sheila I don't care whose it is. Keep your hands off my mother.

Graham Wait a minute. Hold on.

He bellows at the top of his voice as the women struggle

Stop!

They stop. They turn to him

What on earth is going on here? What do you think you're playing at?
You're behaving like a load of kids. You're behaving like a gang of
urchins. There are children in the house. Now stop it. (*He shouts again*) For
Pete's sake stop it and calm down.

They look at one another in shame-faced silence

Ernest enters through the french windows

Ernest (*looking around and beaming*) Not butting in, am I?
Graham What do you want?
Ernest It's the children.
Graham What about the children?
Ernest They're bored. So am I. Can we come in?
Graham Yes, Ernest, yes. You can come in.
Ernest I say, old boy. Excellento. (*Calling into the garden*) You can come in
now. The grown-ups are letting us in.

He stands aside to let in the children. We can't see them, of course

Graham, allow me to introduce you to your children. Well, I know you
already know them, but it's been a long time and——

Graham springs across the room, picks up Julia, kisses her and twirls her round

Graham Julia. How are you, darling? My life, haven't you grown? Quite the
little lady, aren't you? Wowee. (*He puts her down and turns to Crispin*)
Hullo, Crispin. How's it going then, chief? What's that you've got?

Crispin speaks

It's not a weed. It's a delphinium. (*Almost hysterical*) The little swine's
picked one of my prize delphiniums.

Black-out

SCENE 4

The garden. An hour later

*Pamela, Ernest and Graham are playing cricket. The unseen children are
watching. Pamela is batting. Graham bowls to her. She hits the invisible ball
high in the air*

Graham Catch it, Ernest.

Ernest positions himself under the high ball, weaving from side to side

Ernest Right. Right, I've got it.

Graham Mind the cat.
Ernest What?
Graham I said, mind the——

Ernest trips over the cat and falls flat on his back. He lies motionless for a while

Pamela Typical. Absolutely typical.
Graham Are you all right, Ernest? You've not broken anything, have you?
Pamela Of course he's not broken anything. He's just showing off, that's all. Anything to attract attention. Now come on, Ernest, on your feet and let's get on with the game.

Ernest rises slowly to his feet. Then a great grin comes to his face and he holds up his right hand

Ernest Out.
Pamela What?
Ernest You're out. I caught it.
Pamela Typical. Absolutely typical. (*She flings her bat to the ground. Then spins round to the children*) And what you are children laughing at?

Julia speaks

It is not funny, Julia.

Crispin speaks

Don't contradict, Crispin. I said it is not funny. And if I say a thing isn't funny, then, believe you me, young man, it most certainly is not funny.
Graham Come on, come on. Don't squabble. Let's get on with the game. You're batting, Ernest. And you two, on your hind legs and get fielding.

Crispin speaks

Oh yes you are fielding, chief. Listen. You've had your turn batting. Now you've got to do your wack fielding. It's one of life's harsh realities, is that, Crispin. Those who bat must also field.
Ernest Absolutely. Your father's absolutely right there, old chap. That's what makes life so abominably wretched.
Graham Right then, you two—on your feet.

Crispin replies

What do you mean "No"?

Crispin replies

Why?

Crispin replies

Pamela You're bored? Did I hear you say you were bored?

Julia replies

Well, you've no right to be bored, Julia. When I was your age, the word "bored" wasn't allowed to figure in my vocabulary. If ever I used the word "bored" I got hoiked off to bed. Instantly.

Ernest So did I.

Pamela Don't interrupt.

Ernest Sorry.

Pamela Bored! I've never heard anything so preposterous in the whole of my life. These modern children. Everything is put on a plate for them. If you'd been brought up during the war like Uncle Ernest, you'd have . . . Crispin, will you stop picking your nose while I'm talking to you. If you don't want to play cricket, then find something else to do.

Crispin replies

"Such as", Crispin? Such as? Good heavens above, lad, there's everything to do. Gardening. Dress-making. Engine-spotting. Cigarette-card collecting. Why don't you start collecting cigarette cards?

Crispin replies

Yes, Crispin, I know the shops aren't open now. I didn't intend you to . . . I don't know why I'm talking to you like this. Enough. Finished. Off to bed this instant.

Julia replies

Never mind "Flipping heck", Julia. It's long past your bedtime.

Julia replies

It's . . . it's . . . What time is it, Graham?

Graham It's only eight o'clock.

Pamela Only eight o'clock? Good heavens above, when I was their age, I was in bed and fast asleep by half-past seven at the latest.

Graham I know, but they are on holiday, aren't they?

Pamela That is not the point, Graham. The point is that children of their age need, above everything else, adequate sleep. What time do you normally go to bed at home, Julia?

Julia replies

Eleven o'clock? Eleven o'clock? No wonder you're looking so pasty under the eyes.

Crispin replies

Oh yes you are, Crispin. Don't contradict me. I can't stand children who contradict their betters. Children should be seen and not heard.

Ernest I say, Pamela, steady on.

Pamela And the same goes for you.

Ernest Oh Lord.

Pamela What these children need, Graham, is discipline and sleep. And while they're here under my control that is precisely what they are going to get.

Graham Yes, but they are on holiday, Pamela.

Pamela Graham.

Graham Yes, Pamela?

Pamela Did you or did you not ask me to stay with you to help look after your children?

Graham Yes, Pamela.

Pamela Did you or did you not state quite specifically that the reason you needed me was to supply the woman's touch?

Graham Yes.

Pamela Well, that is precisely what I am doing now, Graham. I am supplying the woman's touch to your children. That being the case—bed. Now. No arguments.

Both children reply

No arguments, I said. Come on, we'll go upstairs, and I'll make sure you have a proper bath.

Crispin replies

Crispin, you might have had a bath last Friday, but in this household, young man, we take a bath every day, don't we, Daddy?

Graham (*guiltily*) Pardon?

Pamela I said ... Wait a minute. You didn't have a bath at all yesterday, did you?

Graham Er ... er ... I don't know, Pamela.

Pamela Well, I do. And I'm telling you you didn't. You're beginning to pong, too. You can have a bath tonight after the children are safely tucked in bed. Men! You're worse than children. Right, you two, off you go. Your daddy and Uncle Ernest will be up to say good-night after you've had your bath.

She leads them to the french windows and stops as Crispin speaks

Listen to me, Crispin. I don't care what your grandmother says about too many baths taking the natural oils from your body. You are having a bath and that is that. Now up those stairs. Shoo, shoo. Go on, shoo. (*She drives them in through the french windows, stops and turns to Ernest*) And you can have a bath tonight, too.

Ernest But I had one this morning.

Pamela You have been playing cricket, Ernest. You are dirty. You pong. So you are having a bath and that is that.

Pamela exits through the french windows

Ernest Do you think Don Bradman's wife made him take two baths a day?

Graham Who cares? Come on, let's get on with the game.

Ernest Right. (*He takes up a stance with the bat and speaks in a John Arlott voice*) "And taking up his stance at the Nursery End, it's Ernest Rowley. Just three more runs needed for his double century before lunch as Michael Holding comes swinging in to bowl and——"

He jumps out of the way with a high-pitched scream as Graham hurls a fast ball at him

I say, old boy. Steady on. I'm not wearing a whatsit, you know. You could do a chap a mortal injury hurling a ball around like that.

Pamela (*shouting, off*) Crispin! How dare you. If ever I catch you again doing that with the loofah, I'll . . . I'll . . . Get into that bath. Immediately.

Graham Children! Aren't children bloody?

Ernest Oh, I wouldn't say that, Graham. They can come in jolly useful at times.

Graham Useful? When?

Ernest Well . . . well, when the ball gets lost in the blackberry bushes. Children are damn useful then. You see, they don't mind getting their knees dirty and getting prickled and stung and . . . As a matter of fact, neither do I.

Graham Ernest.

Ernest Yes, old boy?

Graham If you like children all that much, how come you and Pamela never had any?

Ernest Ah. Well, we had a problem, you see.

Graham A problem?

Ernest Yes. A big problem.

Graham Didn't you see the doctor about it?

Ernest Wasn't that sort of problem, old boy.

Graham I see.

Pause

Well, go on. What was the problem?

Ernest Names.

Graham Names?

Ernest Yes. I knew we'd have the most frightful arguments when it came to choosing names for the children. I couldn't bear that. I wasn't worried about sleepless nights and dirty nappies. What worried me was the responsibility of having to choose names. If I had my way, old boy, children wouldn't have names till they grew up. They'd have numbers like soldiers.

Graham laughs

Don't laugh, old boy. I'm serious. I'd much rather have been called seven-seven-four-five-three-oh till I reached the age of puberty and started shaving. I mean, calling me Ernest as a baby has blighted the whole of my life.

Graham How?

Ernest Because I grew up to be like an Ernest. It was expected of me. Think of all the Ernests you know. Bumbling, inconsequential nitwits. Just like me. I couldn't have been anything else. Now, if I'd been called Tex . . .

Graham (*putting his arms round Ernest and hugging him warmly*) I know what you mean, seven-seven-four-five-three-oh. Look at my two. Crispin and Julia. Yuk.

Ernest You didn't choose them, did you?

Graham Good Lord, no. It was Sheila. I'm hopeless at choosing names.

Ernest Really?

Graham Really really. Look at the name I chose for the cat.

Ernest What?

Graham Dobbin. And do you know what the budgie was called before the cat ate it?

Ernest What?

Graham Ramrod.

They laugh and begin to throw the ball to each other

Pamela pokes her head from the bedroom "window"

Pamela You two.

Graham Yes?

Pamela I think it's high time you stopped playing that cricket.

Ernest Flipping heck.

Pamela Never mind "Flipping heck", Ernest. It's half-past eight, and you'll start annoying the neighbours.

Ernest Yes, but——

Pamela Ernest.

Ernest Yes, Pamela?

Pamela Inside and do as you're told.

Pamela disappears inside and slams shut the "window"

Ernest Do you know what I'd like more in the world now, old boy?

Graham What?

Ernest A quick appointment with my dentist.

They stroll in through the french windows arm in arm

SCENE 5

The drawing-room. A few seconds later

Graham and Ernest enter from the garden arm in arm

Ernest I feel really sorry for you, Graham.

Graham Why?

Ernest Having to put up with me and Pamela intruding in your home like this.

Graham You're not intruding, Ernest. I invited you here.

Ernest Bloody fool.

Graham What?

Ernest Fancy inviting me into your home. It's just asking for trouble.

Graham But I like you, Ernest.

Ernest Really?

Graham Of course I like you.

Ernest Really really like me?

Graham Yes, yes. You're one of my best friends.

Ernest *One* of your best friends? A minute ago you said I was your best friend.

Graham All right, all right. You're my best friend.

Ernest Better than all your other best friends?

Graham (*irritably*) Yes, yes. I told you.

Pause

I wish Kate were here.

Ernest So do I.

Graham What?

Ernest She was so beautiful.

Graham Yes.

Ernest Perfect.

Graham Yes.

Ernest Much better than my dentist.

Graham Really?

Ernest Oh yes. And as for the lady from the dog-biscuit shop ...

Graham I loved her.

Ernest I know.

Graham Really loved her. Really, really, really loved her.

Ernest Did she love you?

Graham Oh yes.

Ernest Then why did she walk out on you?

Graham For the same reason that Jane and Belinda walked out on me—the children. They got in the way.

Ernest Poor old Graham.

Graham Children are bloody. They are, aren't they, Ernest? Aren't they, aren't they?

Ernest (*very softly*) She'll come back, Graham. You'll see. She'll come back. I know it. I feel it.

Pause. Then Graham speaks very briskly

Graham I'm dreading this party, you know.

Ernest So am I, old boy. So am I.

He sits at the table. As Graham talks he begins to drive his bus, but it's unobtrusive and in a very low key

Graham When Sheila walked out on me, you know what my only consolation was? I'll tell you. No more children's parties. Imagine it—no more children's parties. The bliss of it. The relief. No more sausages on sticks. No more conjurors drinking whisky out of pink plastic cups. No more mothers with spikey little elbows and spikey little bosoms. No more parcels being passed from sticky hand to sticky hand. No more musical chairs being passed from sticky bottom to sticky bottom. I used to lie awake at nights pouring with sweat just thinking about it. Six months before the party, and I was a quivering wreck. And when it was over, it took another six months to recover from it. My whole life, Ernest, was being blighted by children's parties. My whole existence was being ruined by——

The invisible Crispin enters and utters a piercing, but inaudible "Boo". Ernest and Graham scream with horror and spin round

Crispin! You little swine. Don't you ever do that again. You can give someone a heart attack creeping in like that and shouting "Boo" at the top of your voice. Do that once more, chief, and you're in for a thundering good hiding.

Ernest I say, old boy.

Graham (*angrily*) What do you want?

Ernest It's Crispin.

Graham What about Crispin?

Ernest He's got no togs on.

Graham Oh my God.

Ernest And he's dripping water all over the carpet.

Pamela (*from upstairs, off*) Crispin. Crispin, where are you?

Ernest (*moving across quickly and taking Crispin by the hand*) Come on, old boy. Chaps together. Up the stairs and into bed before she finds out. Women—they're all the same. When you grow up, take a tip from me and don't smoke a pipe. Women always say they like men who smoke pipes. But as soon as you start to smoke it in the old ablutions office, they're down on you like a ton of bricks.

Pamela (*shouting, off*) Crispin. Crispin, come into the bathroom this minute and get yourself talcum powdered.

Ernest Talcum powder. Oh, flipping heck.

Ernest exits with Crispin

Graham pauses. Then begins to walk slowly round the room

Graham Kate. Kate. You're still here, aren't you, Kate? I can hear you. I can smell you. I can feel your touch. Kate. Oh, Kate.

The Lights fade slowly

Scene 6

The children's bedroom. Half an hour later

The room is in darkness. Graham (as Crispin) and Sheila (as Julia) are in the double bed, but unseen at the moment. Pamela and Ernest are standing by the door, illuminated by light from the landing

Pamela They're asleep.

Ernest Yes. Yes. Good old Bedfordshire.

Pamela Don't shout.

Ernest Sorry.

Pamela Would you have liked us to have children, Ernest?

Ernest Beg pardon?

Pamela It's curious. Bathing them and drying them and sprinkling them with talcum powder and tucking them into their bed and seeing them lying there so peaceful and so . . . We could still have children, you know, Ernest?

Ernest What now?

Pamela Don't shout.

Ernest Sorry.

Pamela I'm still young enough to have a child.

Ernest Yes, but . . . but . . .

Pamela But what?

Ernest What the devil are we going to call him?

Pamela What?

Ernest I'm damned if I'm going to have anyone called Wayne or Darren.

Pamela (*laughing softly and snuggling into him*) Oh, Ernest. Oh, Ernest, my darling.

Ernest (*alarmed at this affection*) Beg pardon?

Pamela Shall we? Tonight?

Ernest In someone else's bed?

Pamela Don't shout.

Ernest Sorry.

Pamela (*kissing him again*) Tonight then, Ernest. Tonight.

Pamela leads him away along the landing

The landing light goes off. Darkness. Silence for a moment

Graham (*as Crispin*) Julia. Julia. Are you awake, Julia?

Sheila (*as Julia*) Shut up.

Graham (*as Crispin*) Not until you say if you're awake or not.

Sheila (*as Julia*) Of course I'm awake, you idiot.

Graham (*as Crispin*) Great.

He switches on the light above the bed. They are in a double bed. Graham is sitting up. Sheila is still hidden beneath the sheets

Sheila (*as Julia, still beneath the sheets*) Put that light out.

Graham (*as Crispin*) No.

Sheila (*as Julia*) Crispin, put it out.

Graham (*as Crispin*) Put it out yourself.

Sheila (*as Julia, throwing back the sheets and sitting up in bed*) Right. I will.

She switches off the light. Graham immediately switches it on again. She switches it off. He switches it on

Crispin, they'll hear us.

Graham (*as Crispin*) Won't.

Sheila (*as Julia*) They will.

Graham (*as Crispin*) Won't.

Sheila (*as Julia*) They will.

Pamela (*shouting from downstairs, off*) Stop that talking up there. Settle down and go to sleep.

Sheila (*as Julia*) You see, you see.

She switches off the light. Graham switches it on immediately

Graham (*as Crispin*) I want to wee wee.
Sheila (*as Julia*) No, you don't.
Graham (*as Crispin*) Yes, I do.
Sheila (*as Julia*) You don't. You always say that. You're horrible. I hate you.
Graham (*as Crispin*) I hate you, too. I hate all girls. Girls are rotten. Girls are smelly. Girls are—yar yar yer yar yar.
Pamela (*shouting from downstairs, off*) I won't tell you again. Stop that talking. If I've got to come up there and sort you out, there'll be big trouble. Now go to sleep.
Graham (*as Crispin*) Isn't she awful?
Sheila (*as Julia*) Yuk.
Graham (*as Crispin, mimicking Pamela*) "Shall we, Ernest? Tonight? Tonight, Ernest. Tonight, tonight, tonight."

Sheila giggles

What are they going to do tonight?
Sheila (*as Julia*) Don't you know?
Graham (*as Crispin*) No.
Sheila (*as Julia*) Don't you really know?
Graham (*as Crispin*) No. Tell me.
Sheila (*as Julia*) No.
Graham (*as Crispin*) Tell me, tell me, tell me. (*He wrestles with her and then pinches her*)
Sheila (*as Julia*) Ouch. You pinched me. Stop pinching me.
Graham (*as Crispin*) Well, tell me what they're going to do tonight.
Sheila (*as Julia*) No.
Graham (*as Crispin*) You don't know, do you?
Sheila (*as Julia*) Oh yes I do.
Graham (*as Crispin*) No you don't.
Sheila (*as Julia*) Do.
Graham (*as Crispin*) Don't.
Sheila (*as Julia*) Go to sleep.

She switches off the light. He immediately switches it on again

Graham (*as Crispin*) I hate it here.
Sheila (*as Julia*) So do I.
Graham (*as Crispin*) Why isn't Kate here?
Sheila (*as Julia*) I don't know.
Graham (*as Crispin*) Has she run away like Mummy ran away from Daddy?
Sheila (*as Julia*) I don't know.
Graham (*as Crispin*) Why do men run away from ladies?
Sheila (*as Julia*) I'm not sure. I think it's because they're a different sex.
Graham (*as Crispin*) Ah. You used that word. I'm telling on you.
Sheila (*as Julia*) Don't care.
Graham (*as Crispin*) I like Kate.
Sheila (*as Julia*) So do I.

Graham (*as Crispin*) Kate's terrific at cricket. She doesn't make you field. Not like Daddy. Not like Bruce. Bruce is hopeless at cricket.

Sheila (*as Julia*) Bruce is hopeless at everything. I hate Bruce.

Graham (*as Crispin*) So do I. Hate him, hate him, hate him, hate him.

Pamela (*from downstairs, off*) This is your last warning. If you don't stop talking and go to sleep immediately, I shall be up those stairs and then there'll be tears. Go to sleep. Now. At once.

Silence for a moment

Graham (*as Crispin*) Who's your favourite parent?

Sheila (*as Julia*) My really favourite parent?

Graham (*as Crispin*) Yes. Your really really favourite parent.

Sheila (*as Julia*) I haven't got one.

Graham (*as Crispin*) Neither have I. I think they're both horrible.

Sheila (*as Julia*) Crispin!

Graham (*as Crispin*) Well, they are. They're horrible. And I hate them. Let's run away.

Sheila (*as Julia*) Pardon?

Graham (*as Crispin*) Let's run away. I've got one pound twenty p saved up. We could run away tonight when they're fast asleep. Ernest and Pamela won't know because they'll be doing whatever it is they're going to do and——

Sheila (*as Julia*) We can't run away.

Graham (*as Crispin*) Why not?

Sheila (*as Julia*) Because we've got the party tomorrow.

Graham (*as Crispin*) Oh, flipping heck. I hate parties. I hate them. Hate them, hate them, hate them. (*He climbs out of bed*)

Sheila (*as Julia*) Crispin, what are you doing?

Graham (*as Crispin*) I'm going to look out of the window.

Sheila (*as Julia*) They'll hear you.

Graham (*as Crispin*) They won't.

Sheila (*as Julia*) They will.

Graham (*as Crispin*) Don't care.

Sheila (*as Julia*) Oh, Crispin. You *are* horrible.

Graham (*as Crispin*) I know. (*He draws back the curtain and looks out into the garden*) You know what I'm going to do tomorrow?

Sheila (*as Julia*) What?

Graham (*as Crispin*) I'm going to pull up all his del . . . delph . . . delph . . . I'm going to pull them all up. And I'm going to . . . I'm going to . . . I hate them. Hate them, hate them, hate them.

Pamela (*shouting from downstairs, off*) This is your last and final warning. Any more talking, and I'll send Daddy upstairs to deal with you. And we don't want Daddy up there, do we? Because if Daddy comes up there, Daddy will give us all slap botties, won't he? And we don't want slap botties when we're on holiday, do we? We don't want to fall out with Daddy, when . . . Is someone out of bed?

Graham freezes

Someone's out of bed. It's you, Crispin. I can see you. I'm looking up the chimney and I can see you through the fireplace. Now get back into bed this instant. This instant. Do you hear me? I shall keep looking up that chimney until I see you get back into bed, Crispin.

Graham creeps on tip-toe to the fireplace. He crouches in front of it and sticks out his tongue and leers

Sheila (*as Julia*) Crispin!
Pamela (*from downstairs*) Are you back in bed?
Graham (*as Crispin, shouting downstairs*) Yes.
Pamela (*from downstairs*) Well, go to sleep.
Graham (*as Crispin*) I wish Kate was here.
Sheila (*as Julia*) Well, she isn't, so what's the point in going on about it?
Graham (*as Crispin*) Kate's nice. Kate's pretty. Kate's good fun. Kate's much nicer than Mummy. Much, much, much nicer.

Sheila begins to sob softly

You're crying.
Sheila (*as Julia*) I'm not.
Graham (*as Crispin*) Yes you are.
Sheila (*as Julia*) No I'm not.
Graham (*as Crispin*) Yes you are. (*He tip-toes to the bed. Gently*) Why are you crying, Julia?

Sheila begins to sob uncontrollably. Graham looks at her awkwardly. Awkwardly he reaches out and touches her. She looks up and suddenly smothers him in a passionate hug. Keep it there for a while. Then Graham pulls himself away and coughs with embarrassment. Suddenly he springs back

Who's this, Julia? Who's this? (*He struts up and down the room with his hands behind his back and his chin held high*) "Oh dear, Sheila. Dearie, dearie me. I keep telling you till I'm blue in the face—you're far too soft with those children." Who is it? Who is it, Julia?
Sheila (*as Julia, giggling through her snuffles*) It's Bruce.
Graham (*as Crispin*) Who's this then, Julia? See if you can guess this one. "You've had your turn batting. Now you've got to do your wack fielding. It's one of the harsh realities of life. Those who bat must also field."
Sheila (*as Julia, clapping her hands with delight*) It's Daddy. It's Daddy, it's Daddy.
Pamela (*shouting from downstairs*) Right. That's it. Daddy, will you go upstairs and deal with your children? Thank you.
Sheila (*as Julia*) He's coming. Quick. Into bed.

Graham scampers into bed. Sheila switches off the light

Pamela (*shouting from downstairs*) He's on his way now. I warned you. You took no notice. So now you must pay the penalty. Daddy is now about to deal with you.

Footsteps are heard on the stairs

Sheila (*as Julia, very softly*) I want to go home. I want to go home.

SCENE 7

The drawing-room. Half an hour later

Pamela and Ernest are in their dressing-gowns

Pamela He's been up there a long time.
Ernest Probably fallen asleep.
Pamela What?
Ernest He'll have gone up there, had a good old chin-wag with them, forgotten why he went there in the first place and fallen asleep on the job. That's what I'd have done.
Pamela He's far too soft with those children.
Ernest They're on holiday, Pamela.
Pamela That is not the point, Ernest. Children need to be disciplined. With children you have to be harsh to be kind.
Ernest Like with husbands.
Pamela I beg your pardon?
Ernest Nothing.
Pamela Oh no. You can't get out of it that way, Ernest. What did you just say?
Ernest Nothing. It doesn't matter anyway. Bumbling that's all. I'm always bumbling. I'm that sort of person.
Pamela (*softly*) I like you to bumble, Ernest.
Ernest Beg pardon?
Pamela I like you to bumble and forget things and spill gravy on your cardigan and make a mess of mending the fuse and . . . That's what I like about you, Ernest. That's what I love about you.
Ernest Then why are you always bullying me?
Pamela Because it's the only way I can show how much I love you.
Ernest Beg pardon?
Pamela I need someone to bully, Ernest. I'm that sort of person. Do you understand?
Ernest Yes . . . yes . . . I suppose it's like a good opening batting pair.
Pamela Pardon?
Ernest Well, the best opening pair you can get is a solid defensive right-hander with a graceful attacking left-hander. Opposites, you see. Am I on the right track?
Pamela (*advancing on him*) Oh, Ernest. Oh, Ernest, Ernest. (*She hugs him and kisses him*) Are you ready for bed?
Ernest Ah. Now then. I was meaning to ask you about that. You know what you were saying upstairs there in the children's bedroom?
Pamela Yes.
Ernest Well . . . Well, I don't want to be personal or anything, but did you mean it?
Pamela Why do you ask?
Ernest Well, I've been thinking. You see, if we should . . . you know . . . And,

if we should . . . you know . . . hit the jackpot . . . Well, in nine months' time it's . . . it's . . .

Pamela It's what, Ernest?

Ernest It's the regimental dinner. Well, I never miss the regimental dinner, do I, Pamela?

Pamela Oh, Ernest, Ernest, I do love you. I do, I do. (*She kisses him long and passionately*)

In the middle of this Graham enters in pyjamas and dressing-gown

Graham Oh, sorry, I didn't . . .

Pamela (*spinning round and breaking away from Ernest*) That's quite all right, Graham. Are the children asleep?

Graham Yes.

Pamela And did you punish them?

Graham Well, as a matter of fact, I——

Pamela You didn't, did you? You let them get away with it.

Ernest I say, old girl. Steady on.

Pamela That's quite enough from you. When I want your opinion, I'll ask for it. Until then, kindly keep silent. Keep your nose out of matters you do not understand. Do I make myself clear?

Ernest Yes, yes. Thank goodness for that. Back to the old regime. All that kissing and stuff got me quite worried.

Pamela Be quiet.

Ernest Yes, Pamela.

Pamela Graham, I think you're being very remiss over this matter of discipline. Those children are your flesh and blood and it is your duty as their father to instil in them decent and upright standards of behaviour.

Graham Pamela.

Pamela Yes?

Graham Pamela, let me tell you what happened when I went upstairs. My children were awake. I talked to them. I cuddled them in my arms. I stroked their hair. They fell asleep. And I sat there on the bed looking at them. And I saw myself. I saw myself in Julia. I saw myself in Crispin. The two parts of me. I looked at them long and hard, Pamela. And all of a sudden I felt lonely. I felt desolate. I felt totally and completely and utterly lonely.

Pamela I see. So what you're saying is that you want Sheila back.

Graham No, Pamela. No, no, no. I am not saying that. I do not want Sheila back. I want Kate back. (*Shouting*) I want Kate back in this house. Now.

Silence. Then faintly from upstairs.

Sheila (*as Julia, off*) Daddy. Daddy, Daddy.

They freeze. Then more loudly

Daddy, Daddy, Daddy.

Graham (*dashing to the door*) Yes, Julia? What do you want?

Sheila (*as Julia, off*) I want to go home, Daddy. I want to go home. Now.

BLACK-OUT

ACT II

SCENE 1

The garden. The following day. Mid-morning

Graham is looking at the privet bush trying to make up his mind about plucking a leaf. He takes courage, plucks one, folds it carefully, dampens it and blows. A thin rasp comes from it. He beams. He tries again and out comes a raspy National Anthem

Graham I can do it. Wayhay. I can do it.

He races in through the french windows crying out in triumph

SCENE 2

The drawing-room. A few seconds later

Ernest is reading his newspaper

Graham enters through the french windows, brandishing his leaf and crying in triumph

Graham I can do it. I can do it, Ernest.
Ernest (*looking up from his paper grumpily*) Do what?
Graham Blow a tune through a privet leaf.
Ernest Oh that. (*He goes back to his paper*)
Graham (*pulling back Ernest's paper*) No, listen. Go on, listen. Be a sport, Ernest. What's this? See if you can guess. (*He blows the leaf. A very raspy National Anthem is produced. He smiles in triumph*) Well? What is it?
Ernest Haven't a clue, old boy.

Ernest returns to his paper. Graham pulls it back

Graham It's *God Save The Queen*.
Ernest That?
Graham Yes.
Ernest Rubbish.
Graham Oh, it's rubbish, is it?
Ernest Absolutely.
Graham All right, then, clever dick, let's see what you can do. You've been bragging about what you can do. Well, come on then—let's see what you're made of.
Ernest All right. I will.

He takes the privet leaf and blows. Nothing happens. Graham starts to laugh.
As his laughter increases so does Ernest blow more violently and with total lack
of success

Graham You see, you see. You can't even produce a squeak.

Ernest And do you know why?

Graham Because you're hopeless.

Ernest No. It is not because I am hopeless, Graham. It is because this is not
my privet leaf.

Graham What?

Ernest This is your privet leaf. You chose it to your specifications. You
tailored it to suit your requirements. And, therefore, only you can play it.
A privet leaf is a precision instrument that can only be played by one
person. (*He picks up his paper and rustles it angrily*)

Graham You're in a bad mood this morning.

Ernest No, I'm not.

Graham Yes you are. What's the matter with you? Ah, I know. All that
kissing and cuddling with Pamela last night led to better things, didn't it?

Ernest No it did not. Pamela's not that sort of person. Thank goodness.

Graham Well, then why are you in a bad mood?

Ernest I'm not.

Graham You are.

Ernest I'm not, I'm not, I'm not. All right. I'll tell you why I'm in a bad
mood. It's this children's party.

Graham Oh that.

Ernest When I agreed to come here and help you out, Graham, I'd no idea
there was going to be a children's party.

Graham Neither had I.

Ernest I thought it would be a simple case of Pamela dashing hither and
thither, harrying and bullying and thwacking to her heart's content, and
you and I would be sitting in the garden drinking snorters and doing sports
quizzes.

Graham That's what I thought, too.

Ernest But a children's party, old boy. Really. It's too bad.

Graham Let's run away.

Ernest Beg pardon?

Graham There's still time. The party doesn't start for another couple of
hours. We can sneak out through the garden, creep down the snicket
and——

Ernest And into the pub and three solid hours of snorters. Excellento. A1
idea, old boy.

Graham I don't mean that.

Ernest No?

Graham No. We run away for good.

Ernest Beg pardon?

Graham The open road, Ernest. It beckons. Adventures. Exotic tropic
islands. Swaying palms. Sensuous dusky native girls. Wild dancing women

with … with … (*He droops his shoulders*) Anything interesting in the paper?

Ernest Not really. There's been an earthquake in Turkey. Eight dead.

Graham Oh dear.

Ernest It'll rise to about five thousand. It always does.

Graham Yes.

Ernest I always feel so guilty about it.

Graham What?

Ernest Totting up the numbers. It's the same with the unemployment figures.

Graham What is?

Ernest The guilt. I don't want them to rise. But every month, when they're announced I say to myself: "Come on, you can get to a million, if you try. Just a bit more effort all round and you can beat the record. Come on, chaps, all pull together. Let's have that record." I'm that sort of chap. Any kind of record cheers me up.

They turn to the french windows as Crispin and Julia enter

Graham Hullo, kids. Gosh, you look miserable. What's the matter with you?

Crispin replies

Neither do we, chief. A children's party's the last thing we want.

Julia speaks

Because … because. Well, because—that's why.

Ernest That's no answer, old boy.

Graham No? Well, what is the answer?

Ernest We're having a children's party, because Pamela wants a children's party. It's not for our benefit, Graham. It's not for your benefit, Julia and Crispin. It's for Pamela. More people to boss. More people to bully. More people to make miserable and wretched.

Crispin speaks

So do I, old chap. I want to go home just as much as you do.

Graham You are not going home. No-one's going home.

Julia speaks

Because, Julia, the judge says you've got to spend your holidays with me. It's all a question of access.

Julia speaks

Access? Well, it means, whether you like it or I like it, you've got to spend part of each year with me.

Crispin speaks

I don't care whether you like it, Crispin. It's the judge. Blame the bloody judge. He's the one who started all this. That big fat swine sitting on his bench with his silly wig and his——

Crispin speaks

What's that?

Crispin speaks again. Graham's shoulders droop

I don't know where Kate is, Crispin.

Julia speaks

She didn't tell me, Julia. When she walked out on me she just . . . I don't know where she is, Julia.

Julia speaks

Of course, Julia. I'd like Kate to be here just as much as you.

Crispin speaks

Yes, Crispin. Yes, yes, yes. It *was* nice when Kate was here.

Julia speaks

Yes, Julia. Yes, yes, yes, yes. She *is* beautiful. She's beautiful, she's tender, she's romantic, she's passionate and (*screaming*) I don't know where she is.

Pause

Pamela enters, bearing at arm's length a very dirty sock

Pamela I found this on the bathroom floor. All right—whose is it? Crispin? Julia?

Graham It's mine.

Pamela I see. Well, what do we do with our dirty socks, Graham? We don't leave them lying around on the bathroom floor, do we? We bring them downstairs and we put them in the washing-machine. Right, Graham, right?

Graham Right, Pamela.

Pamela And what are you two children laughing at?

Crispin speaks

Well, Crispin, if you're laughing at nothing, there must be something radically wrong with you, that's all I can say. Maybe you need a good dose of bed to cure you.

Ernest I say. Steady on, old girl.

Pamela Oh, you've piped up now, have you? Wait a minute. Come here. Come on.

Ernest slopes over to her

Mouth open.

Ernest opens his mouth

I thought so. You haven't cleaned your teeth this morning, have you?

Ernest I can't remember.

Pamela Oh yes you can. You haven't cleaned your teeth, have you? I can see bits of marmalade stuck in them.

Ernest I know. That's because I've had my brekker since I cleaned my teeth.

Pamela Oh I see. So we only clean our teeth once a day, do we? It doesn't matter how dirty they get, we only ... I will not tell you children again. Stop laughing. Good heavens above, you're having your party in half an hour's time. You can't afford to stand about laughing. There's work to be done. Now get yourselves up to that bathroom, give yourselves a good scrub and change into those clothes I've put out on your bed. And you can do the same, Ernest.

Ernest What?

Pamela Upstairs to your bedroom. Clean your teeth. Wash and shave. And you've a clean shirt hanging in the wardrobe.

Ernest Flipping heck, what a life. Come on, kids. Last one to the airing cupboard's a cissy.

Ernest exits into the hall with the children

Pamela turns to Graham. He is staring at her intently. It discomforts her

Pamela (*holding up the sock rather nervously*) This is yours, I believe.

Graham That's right, Pamela.

Pamela (*handing it to him*) Here.

Graham Thank you, Pamela. (*He stuffs it into his pocket and stares at her intently*)

Pause

Pamela I don't like being a bully, you know.

Graham Really?

Pamela When I was a child, I was very shy.

Graham Were you?

Pamela Painfully shy. It says so on my school reports.

Graham Ah. Then that's conclusive.

Pamela I hated parties. I never knew what to say. I always felt I was being stared at. I used to skulk in corners, but I always felt everyone was looking at me. I hated it. I could never eat any food. I had this nervous tummy, and I couldn't get anything past my lips.

Graham Poor old you.

Pamela So I decided to change. When I reached "that certain age", I made a conscious decision to change my whole personality. I thought about it for ages and ages. What should I become? A vamp? A flirt? A scatter-brain? A blue-stocking frump? They all had their attractions, but ... But a bully, Graham, a bully is really something. Everyone notices you. Everyone talks about you. You don't have to skulk. You don't have to hide. So, I thought to myself: Right, I'll be a bully. And overnight I changed. I bullied my mother. I bullied my father. I bullied my friends. And it worked. They were all so shocked, they gave into me. Lovely power I had. Lovely. And then I met Ernest. He loves me for being a bully, and so I'm stuck with being a bully. If I didn't bully him, he'd go to pieces. There'd be no Ernest. And without Ernest, there'd be no me. I love Ernest. (*She pauses. Then firmly*) I love Ernest to distraction.

Graham smiles. He walks to her and kisses her lightly on top of the head

Graham I'll go up and get changed.

   He exits through the hall door

Pamela begins to tidy up the room, punching cushions etc. She turns and trips over the cat

Pamela That cat. Get out of the way. Get out of my—— (*She stops dead, smiles and crouches on her knees*) Here, puss. Puss, puss, puss, puss. (*She picks it up and rubs her cheek against it*) There, there, there. Who's a lovely puss-cat? I love you, puss-cat. I do. Pamela loves you.

SCENE 3

The children's bedroom. A little later

Sheila as Julia is putting on her frock—it is an adult's frock, by the way

Graham as Crispin enters. He looks at her silently for a moment

Graham (*as Crispin*) I gobbed in the bath.
Sheila (*as Julia*) Crispin. You shouldn't use that word. It's awful.
Graham (*as Crispin*) Gob, gob, gob, gob.
Sheila (*as Julia*) You're being silly.
Graham (*as Crispin*) Gob, gob, gob, gob.
Sheila (*as Julia*) It's not clever. It's very rude.

Graham goes to the window and looks out

   I bet you didn't wash your neck properly. She'll kill you if she finds another tide-mark.
Graham (*as Crispin*) Someone's coming.
Sheila (*as Julia*) What?
Graham (*as Crispin*) It's a kid coming to the party.
Sheila (*as Julia, rushing to the window*) Let's have a look. Budge up, Crispin. Ugh. Yuk.
Graham (*as Crispin*) Isn't she awful?
Sheila (*as Julia*) Horrible. Terrible. Yuk.

Graham pulls a face at the girls outside

Graham (*as Crispin*) Yar yar yer yar yar.
Sheila (*as Julia*) Crispin, don't. (*She pulls him away from the window*)
Graham (*as Crispin*) I hate Pamela. (*Mimicking her*) "What do we do with our dirty socks, Graham? We don't leave them lying around on the bathroom floor, do we? We bring them downstairs and we put them in the washing-machine. Right, Graham, right?" I hate her.
Sheila (*as Julia*) You shouldn't use the word "hate". It's rude.
Graham (*as Crispin*) Why don't we burn the house down?
Sheila (*as Julia*) What?

Graham (*as Crispin*) You shouldn't use the word "what". It's rude. You should say pardon.

Sheila (*as Julia*) Never mind that. What do you mean about burning the house down?

Graham (*as Crispin*) We should burn the house down so we don't have to go to the party.

Sheila (*as Julia*) You're being silly again.

Graham (*as Crispin*) I'm not.

Sheila (*as Julia*) You are.

Graham (*as Crispin*) I hate you.

Sheila (*as Julia*) And I hate you.

Graham (*as Crispin*) I'd give anything not to go to this party.

Sheila (*as Julia*) So would I.

Graham (*as Crispin*) I'd give up . . . I'd give up my Liverpool scarf. I'd give up . . . I'd give up getting a terrapin for Christmas. I'd give up——

Sheila (*as Julia*) There is a way.

Graham (*as Crispin*) Pardon?

Sheila (*as Julia*) I've thought of a way of not going to the party.

Graham (*as Crispin*) How?

Sheila (*as Julia*) Ring up Mummy.

Graham (*as Crispin*) Ring up Mummy?

Sheila (*as Julia*) We ring up Mummy and tell her that we're having a lousy, rotten old time, and we want to come home. She'd be round for us like a shot.

Graham (*as Crispin*) Yes.

Sheila (*as Julia*) She always wants us to have a rotten time here. She always asks us and she's always disappointed, if we say we've enjoyed ourselves.

Graham (*as Crispin*) Yes, yes. We'll tell her we want her to come round right away. Today.

Sheila (*as Julia*) I've thought of something even better. Heaps and heaps better.

Graham (*as Crispin*) What?

Sheila (*as Julia*) We'll tell her that it's Pamela who's making us miserable.

Graham (*as Crispin*) Brill. She hates Pamela.

Sheila (*as Julia*) We'll tell her that Pamela's bullying us and hitting us and making us cry.

Graham (*as Crispin*) Yes, yes. Brill.   •

Sheila (*as Julia*) And then you tell her——

Graham (*as Crispin*) I tell her?

Sheila (*as Julia*) Yes.

Graham (*as Crispin*) I'm not telling her.

Sheila (*as Julia*) Yes you are.

Graham (*as Crispin*) No I'm not. You are. It's your idea so it's only fair you ring Mummy up.

Sheila (*as Julia*) Listen to me, Crispin. I'm older than you. And I know—you are a much better liar than me.

Graham (*as Crispin, with delight*) Honestly?

Sheila (*as Julia*) Course you are. You're heaps and heaps better than me at lying. I couldn't lie to Mummy. But you could. You'd make it sound so true. You always do when you tell fibs.

Graham (*as Crispin*) Honestly?

Sheila (*as Julia*) Honestly. Cross my heart. You're the best liar in the whole of the wide world.

Graham (*as Crispin*) OK. OK. I'll do it. (*Rehearsing*) Mummy, Mummy, we want to go home. Pamela's hitting us all the time. I've got a terrific bruise on my botty and she's pulling Julia's hair all the time and twisting her arm and I'm frightened, Mummy. Mummy, Mummy, you've got to come round and bring us home straight away.

Sheila (*as Julia, clapping her hands with delight*) Yes. Yes, that's it, Crispin. Terrific.

Graham (*as Crispin*) Right. I'll go now.

Sheila (*as Julia*) Be careful, Crispin. Don't let anyone see you.

Graham (*as Crispin*) Right. I'll be really really careful. Mummy, Mummy, Mummy, we want to go home.

Graham exits

Sheila hugs herself with delight

SCENE 4

The drawing-room. Half an hour later

Ernest is sitting at the table driving his bus

Graham enters with the phone in his hand

Graham It's all hell out there, Ernest.

Ernest I bet it is, old boy.

Graham Hundreds of screaming kids. Thousands of them. Pamela dashing round thwacking them and stuffing them with sausages. Murder. Good God, I've just caught Crispin on the phone jabbering away like a dervish.

Ernest I say.

Graham That's why I've brought it in. Kids and telephones—lethal combination, Ernest. Leave a telephone with a child and next thing you know it's made half a dozen long distance calls to Australia and ordered you three video machines from Radio Rentals. (*He puts the phone on the floor and wags a finger at it*) Now stay there. Sit. I don't want a peep out of you for the next five hours.

Immediately the phone rings. He lashes out at it with his foot but misses

Ernest I say, old boy. Steady on.

Graham I will not steady on. I warned it. I will not tolerate disobedience. I will be master in my own house. I will ... Oh, blast it. (*He picks up the receiver and snaps*) Hullo. Who's that? ... My name, madam, is Graham Carey ... Yes, yes, there is a children's party taking place. The house is now under a state of siege. I'm expecting the SAS to arrive very shortly with machine pistols and percussion grenades and—— Don't you talk to me like that, madam. Who are you anyway? . . . Oh. Oh, I see. Well, it's not that bad. I was only joking. It's tremendous really. We're all having great fun. Tinkle of happy laughter and . . . Whose mummy are you? . . . James Delaney's mother. I see . . . Yes, yes . . . Yes. Yes, I'll tell him that, Mrs Delaney. You can rely on me. Bye. Thanks for calling. (*He puts down the phone, goes to the hall door and shouts*) Is there a James Delaney in the house? Paging James Delaney. James Delaney, there is a message for you in the drawing-room.

The invisible James Delaney enters

James Delaney?

James Delaney speaks

Well then, James Delaney, I have just spoken to your mother on the telephone. She tells me that you are not to eat any blancmange as it makes you sick. Right then, James Delaney, bearing that in mind I intend to get sticking tape and——

James Delaney speaks

You've already had blancmange?

James Delaney speaks

And you've already been sick. Good. And where, James Delaney, have you been sick?

James Delaney speaks

And what did the cat do?

James Delaney speaks

Yes, well, James Delaney, cats are like that. Cats are almost human in their aversion to little boys. Cats are—— (*He screams*) Don't be sick here. Quick. In the garden. (*He grabs hold of the invisible James Delaney, drags him across the room and boots him out through the french windows*) Do it out there. Oh no. Not there. Those are my prize delphiniums. (*He slams the french windows*) Oh Lord. Did we behave like that when we were children, Ernest?

Ernest Oh yes.

Graham And did we survive?

Ernest Oh yes. You should see us now.

Graham I hated parties when I was a child.

Ernest So did I.

Graham Really?

Ernest Loathed them, old boy. Sheer purgatory.

Graham Why?

Ernest Well, you see, old boy, being the type of child I was—dull, stupid, clumsy, a congenital bumbler—well, people always expected me to play the fool. "Come on, Ernest," they'd say. "Do your party piece." And I'd do my party piece. Fall off the chair.

Graham Fall off a chair?

Ernest Yes. I must hold the world junior record for falling off chairs. No wonder I've grown up to be like I am now—dull, stupid, clumsy, a congenital bumbler, always forgetting to do the old flies up. (*He looks down and sees his trousers are undone*) You see. What did I tell you? (*He hastily adjusts his flies*)

As he does so, Pamela enters bearing on a tray a bottle of sherry and three glasses

Pamela I see, Ernest. Forgotten to do our flies up again, have we?

Ernest Oh, Pamela, don't go on at me like that. I'm too old to change now and ... (*He spots the bottle*) What's that?

Pamela I've brought us a drink.

Graham What?

Pamela Graham, I wish you wouldn't keep saying "What". Pardon is the word we use. Pardon.

Graham Pardon.

Pamela Thank you. I was saying that I've brought us all a drink. Dry sherry. Yes?

Graham Yes, please. I should say so.

Pamela You, too, Ernest?

Ernest Ra-ther. Excellento. What ... what's brought all this on?

Pamela All what on, Ernest?

Ernest Drinky poos.

Pamela It's a reward.

Graham For what?

Pamela For all the work we've done.

Ernest But Graham and I haven't done any work, Pamela. We've kept out of your way. Specifically.

Pamela Exactly. And it's because you've kept out of my way that we're having a drink.

Ernest Beg pardon?

Pamela I didn't want you to help, you big booby.

Ernest Oh.

Pamela When I arrange something, Ernest, I carry it through myself. If I want help, I ask for it. I did not want your help, so I did not ask for it. It's a lesson we have to learn when we're grown up, isn't it? Never start something you can't finish. Am I right, Graham?

Graham Absolutely.

Pamela Good. Ernest, will you pour?

Ernest Certainly. But what about the hordes outside?

Pamela Everything is taken care of, Ernest. They've been fed and watered. They're contented. They're in the lounge enjoying themselves. When I've had this drink, I shall go into the lounge and see how they are progressing. Until that time we have a drink. And we relax. (*She laughs*) You silly boys. All that fuss you made about the party. There was no need to, was there? You made a fuss about nothing. Relax. Enjoy yourselves. Enjoy yourselves like the children enjoying themselves in the lounge.

Graham and Ernest look at each other slightly bewildered. Pamela laughs loud and long

SCENE 5

The drawing-room. A few seconds later

All the adults are children. Graham is Crispin, Sheila is Julia, Ernest is the young Ernest, Pamela is the young Pamela, Mrs Mitten is her younger gawky self. They are sitting in the lounge looking infinitely gloomy. Silence for a while

Sheila (*as Julia*) Well, what do we do now?

Graham (*as Crispin*) She said we'd got to enjoy ourselves.

Mrs Mitten (*as child*) That's all very well. But how do we enjoy ourselves, if we're not told how to?

Graham (*as Crispin*) Ugh. Isn't she a drip?

Mrs Mitten (*as child*) I'm not a drip. You shouldn't talk to me like that any road. I'm older than what you are.

Sheila (*as Julia*) "Older than what you are"? What way's that to speak? Ooh, isn't she common? Hasn't she got a horrible accent?

Mrs Mitten (*as child*) I haven't.

Sheila (*as Julia*) You have.

Mrs Mitten (*as child*) I haven't.

Sheila (*as Julia*) Oh yes you have. You don't sound your aitches.

Mrs Mitten (*as child, bursting into tears*) I can't help it. We've just moved here. I want to go home.

Graham (*as Crispin*) Oh, shut up. (*He screams at her*) Shut up.

She stops. There is silence for a moment

All right. Who's going to be the first to enjoy himself?

Ernest (*as child*) Oh dear. Oh dear, here we go again. (*With great solemnity and very slowly he falls off the chair*)

Sheila (*as Julia*) Do it again.

Ernest (*as child*) If you give me a kiss.

Sheila (*as Julia*) No.

Graham (*as Crispin*) Go on. Give him a kiss. With a bit of luck he'll break his neck next time.

Ernest (*as child*) Oh no I won't.

Graham (*as Crispin*) Oh yes you will. Bet you.

Ernest (*as child*) Bet me what?

Graham (*as Crispin*) Bet you my Liverpool track-suit.

Ernest (*as child*) No.

Graham (*as Crispin*) Why not?

Ernest (*as child*) Because I don't like football that's why.

Mrs Mitten (*as child*) Neither do I.

Sheila (*as Julia*) Shut up. (*To Ernest*) Look, you, Thingie.

Ernest (*as child*) Ernest. That's what my name is. Ernest.

Graham (*as Crispin*) Ernest? Yar yar yer yar yar.

They all laugh

Ernest (*as child*) What's the matter? What are you laughing at?

Graham (*as Crispin*) Your name. It's a daft name. Ernest is a daft, soppy, weedy name.

Pamela (*as child. She is, of course, very quiet and shy*) I don't think it is.

Graham (*as Crispin*) Oh, she's spoken.

Sheila (*as Julia*) Wonders never cease. She's got a tongue. Come on then, show us. Show us your tongue.

She and Graham chant "Show us your tongue, show us your tongue"

Pamela (*as child*) Leave me alone.

Ernest (*as child*) Yes. Leave her alone.

Graham (*as Crispin*) Ah. He loves her.

Ernest (*as child*) I don't.

Graham (*as Crispin*) Yes, you do. You love her. You love her, you love her, you love her. Go on. Give her a kiss.

Ernest (*as child*) No.

Graham (*as Crispin*) You're scared.

Ernest (*as child*) I'm not.

Graham (*as Crispin*) You are. You're a scaredy cat. Scaredy, scaredy, scaredy cat.

Sheila (*as Julia*) Oh, shut up, Crispin. Don't be such a baby. Look, you. If I kiss you, will you promise to fall off the chair again?

Ernest (*as child*) Yes.

Sheila (*as Julia*) Right. Sit still.

She kisses him. Immediately he falls off the chair

Mrs Mitten (*as child*) I think you're all daft. I think you're barmy. I want to go home.

Sheila (*as Julia*) Well, go home then.

Mrs Mitten (*as child*) I can't.

Sheila (*as Julia*) Why not?

Mrs Mitten (*as child*) Because I can't.

Sheila (*as Julia*) Why?

Mrs Mitten (*as child*) Because ... because ... because my mum's out at work and there's no-one at home.

Graham (*as Crispin*) Ugh. Does your mummy go out to work?

Mrs Mitten (*as child*) Yes.

Graham (*as Crispin*) Ugh. Her mummy has to go out to work because they're so poor and——

Mrs Mitten (*as child*) We're not poor. We've got an automatic Volvo. We're no more poorer than what you are. We're richer than what you are.

Sheila (*as Julia*) Then why does your mummy have to go out to work?

Mrs Mitten (*as child*) Because I haven't got a dad, that's why.

Graham (*as Crispin*) She hasn't got a dad. Yar yar yer yar yar.

Ernest (*as child*) I say.

Sheila (*as Julia*) What?

Ernest (*as child*) Let's pull her hair.

Graham (*as Crispin*) Yeah. Let's pull her hair. Come on, everyone, let's pull her hair and kick her.

Ernest (*as child*) Let's pull her knickers down.

Graham (*as Crispin*) Yeah, yeah. Let's pull her knickers down.

They crowd round her. Graham pulls her hair and Ernest struggles to pull her knickers down. She screams and shouts. Pamela stands shyly in the background. Finally Mrs Mitten breaks free, sobbing

Mrs Mitten (*as child*) Right then. Right. I'm telling on you. I'm telling.

She flees from the room, screaming as they advance on her

SCENE 6

The drawing-room. A few seconds later

Ernest, Pamela and Graham are contentedly drinking sherry. The hall door is open

Graham It's so pleasant. All nice and quiet and peaceful and——

They all spin round as the invisible Mrs Mitten comes charging through the door

Pamela What on earth are you doing in here? I thought I told you children were confined to the lounge and the garden and——

Mrs Mitten tries to speak through her tears

If you'd stop crying, my dear, I might be able to understand you.

Mrs Mitten tries again

Stop crying. Stop it at once.

Mrs Mitten stops

Right. Now what's the matter?

Mrs Mitten speaks

Who pulled your hair?

Mrs Mitten speaks

Crispin. I see. Well, if he pulled your hair, he must have had a reason for doing it, mustn't he? And, in any case, my dear, when we're at a party we don't tell tales on the other guests, do we? (*To Ernest and Graham*) Ugh. Isn't she a common little thing? That accent. And that frock. She looks as though she's been dragged through a——

Mrs Mitten speaks

He did what?

Mrs Mitten speaks

Who did? Who tried to pull your knickers down?

Mrs Mitten speaks

The little fat boy? Right. Right then, leave this to me. (*She takes Mrs Mitten by the hand and leads her to the hall door. She pauses*) Pulling knickers. Whatever next?

Pamela exits

Pause

Ernest I once pulled down a girl's knickers at a party.
Graham Oh yes?
Ernest Esme Pearson.
Graham Pardon?
Ernest Esme Pearson. That's the girl whose knickers I pulled down. Well, I didn't actually pull them down all the way. As a matter of fact I hardly pulled them down at all. I'm that sort of person.

As he is talking, Graham's attention is attracted by an invisible child who is wandering round the garden and then begins to approach the french windows. Graham is utterly transfixed by the approaching child and totally ignores Ernest

She married an estate agent. He had great hairy legs, if memory serves me correct. Well, so did Esme as a matter of fact. They were a damn good match on that score. They went to live in Uganda. You wouldn't think there was much call for estate agents in Uganda, would you? That's probably why they came back. Yes, they came back and went to live in Basingstoke. Or was it Barrow-on-Soar? It could have been ...
Graham (*to the invisible child who is standing at the french windows*) Yes? What do you want?

Ernest turns to her

Ernest I say, old boy. I say.
Graham Don't be shy. Tell us what you want.

The girl speaks

Yes, there is a party here. It started ages and ages ago.
Ernest I say, what a beautiful little girl.
Graham Isn't she just. Gorgeous. She's absolutely——

The girl speaks

Yes, you can cut through here. They're in the lounge, I think. Tell you what, I'll take you in and introduce you. Would you like that?

The girl speaks

Good. Well, I'd better know your name then, hadn't I?

The girl speaks

What?

The girl speaks

Kate? Your name is Kate?

Black-out

SCENE 7

The drawing-room. A few minutes later

Graham as Crispin is there with Kate. Kate is adult, of course, but acts as a child

Kate (*as child*) So you're Crispin?
Graham (*as Crispin*) Yes.
Kate (*as child*) I'm Kate.
Graham (*as Crispin*) I know. Daddy just told me.
Kate (*as child*) I like your daddy.
Graham (*as Crispin*) What?
Kate (*as child*) I like your daddy.
Graham (*as Crispin*) Do you know him?
Kate (*as child*) No.
Graham (*as Crispin*) Then how can you like him?
Kate (*as child*) Because I can, that's why.
Graham (*as Crispin*) I think you're daft. I'm going out to play cricket with
the others.
Kate (*as child*) I love your daddy.
Graham (*as Crispin, stopping dead in his tracks*) You love my daddy?
Kate (*as child*) Yes.
Graham (*as Crispin*) Really really?
Kate (*as child*) Yes.
Graham (*as Crispin*) Really really really?
Kate (*as child*) Yes. I love your daddy very much.
Graham (*as Crispin*) Why do you love him very much?
Kate (*as child*) He's nice.
Graham (*as Crispin*) How do you know he's nice?
Kate (*as child*) Because I watch him.
Graham (*as Crispin*) Where?
Kate (*as child*) For your information I live in the big house with the green
roof. My bedroom overlooks your house. I sit there and watch your daddy.
Graham (*as Crispin*) Where?
Kate (*as child*) I watch him when he's in the garden. He looks nice.
Graham (*as Crispin*) Why does he look nice?
Kate (*as child*) He's got a nice face.
Graham (*as Crispin*) He hasn't.
Kate (*as child*) He has.

Graham (*as Crispin*) Oh no he hasn't. My daddy's got a face that's ugly as . . . that's ugly as . . . that's as ugly as anything.

Kate (*as child*) I think you're a very silly little boy.

Graham (*as Crispin*) I'll punch you in the teeth.

Kate (*as child*) Boys don't punch girls.

Graham (*as Crispin*) Don't care.

Kate (*as child, mocking him*) "Don't care, don't care, don't care." Who would ever think you were the son of your daddy?

Graham (*as Crispin*) Pardon?

Kate (*as child*) You look like your daddy. You've got a nice face like your daddy. You walk like your daddy. You've got the same colour eyes. And the same mouth. And the same nice hair. But you don't act like your daddy one little bit.

Graham (*as Crispin*) Oh yes I do.

Kate (*as child*) No you don't.

Graham (*as Crispin*) Well, how does Daddy act, clever dick?

Kate (*as child*) He's kind. He's loving. He's funny. He's just . . . he's just nice.

Graham (*as Crispin*) No he's not. He's rotten. My daddy's rotten. He's not nice. He's not kind. He's horrible and he's cruel and he hits us all the time and that's why my mummy's coming to take us home. She's coming to take us home today because my daddy's been beating us up all the time. I hate my daddy. Hate him, hate him, hate him.

Kate (*as child*) How old are you?

Graham (*as Crispin*) Not telling.

Kate (*as child*) You're eight.

Graham (*as Crispin*) I'm not.

Kate (*as child*) Oh yes you are.

Graham (*as Crispin*) Oh no I'm not. I'm eight and a half.

Kate (*as child*) I'm older than you.

Graham (*as Crispin*) You're not as old as my sister.

Kate (*as child*) How old's your sister?

Graham (*as Crispin*) Not telling. I'm going to play cricket. (*He moves to the door*)

Kate (*as child*) I'd like to live in this house.

Graham (*as Crispin, stopping dead*) What?

Kate (*as child*) I love this house.

Graham (*as Crispin*) You've never been in it before.

Kate (*as child*) I love this house. It's a nice house. It's a friendly house. There's a lot of love in this house.

Graham (*as Crispin*) You've never been in it before.

Kate (*as child*) How do you know, little boy?

Graham (*as Crispin*) Don't call me "little boy".

Kate (*as child*) Why? Don't you like it, little boy?

Graham (*as Crispin*) I'll kick you.

Kate (*as child*) Little boy, if you kick me, I'll kick you back so hard you'll end up in the middle of next week.

Graham (*as Crispin*) Go on then. Kick me. Go on, kick me, kick me.

Kate (*as child*) Come here, little boy.

Graham (*as Crispin*) Pardon?
Kate (*as child*) I said, little boy—come here. Come on. Come to me, little
  boy.

He hesitates. He moves to her

  Here you are, little boy. This is just for you.

He flinches, but she embraces him and kisses him long and hard

  There. That was nice, wasn't it, little boy? Shall we go out and play cricket?

The Lights fade to a Black-out

SCENE 8

The garden. A few minutes later

*Ernest, Sheila and Mrs Mitten as children are playing cricket. Pamela as a
child stands shyly on her own. Ernest is running up to bowl to Mrs Mitten when
he spots Pamela. He stops*

Ernest (*as child*) Are you playing or aren't you?
Pamela (*as child*) Yes.
Sheila (*as Julia*) Yes what? Yes, you're playing? Or yes, you're not playing?
Pamela (*as child*) Yes, I'm playing.
Ernest (*as child*) Well, start fielding then.

Shyly Pamela begins to walk towards him

  Not there. There. What a drip. You're a drip, you are.
Mrs Mitten (*as child*) Are you going to bowl or not?
Ernest (*as child*) Yes, I'm going to bowl. I'm going to bowl one so fast, it'll
  break your nose.
Mrs Mitten (*as child, throwing down the bat*) Not playing then.
Sheila (*as Julia*) Cowardy, cowardy custard.
Ernest }
Sheila } (*together, as children*) Blah blah bler blah blah.

*Kate as a child and Graham as Crispin enter from round the side of the house.
Kate is holding his hand. They stand watching them in silence*

  Blah blah bler blah blah. Blah blah bler blah blah.
Mrs Mitten (*as child*) You think you're right clever, don't you?
Sheila (*as Julia*) "Right clever"? "Right clever"? Do you mean "really
  clever"?
Ernest (*as child*) Isn't she common? Yerrrrk. Isn't she frightful?
Kate (*as child*) I think she's rather nice.

They turn to her. She walks to Mrs Mitten

I think you're rather nice. (*She looks her up and down*) Yes. Yes, you are rather nice.

The others stare at her silently

Well, go on, little boy. Aren't you going to play cricket with your little friends?

They are all stock still and silent. She pushes Graham forward

Go on, little boy. Play. Play with your little friends.

Graham walks over to them. He picks up the bat

Graham (*as Crispin, softly*) Shall I bat?
Ernest (*as child, softly, too*) Yes. You bat. I'll bowl.
Mrs Mitten (*as child, very softly*) Can I be backstop?
Sheila (*as Julia, softly*) Yes. You can be backstop. I'll field.

It is almost dream-like as they start to play. It should be done as quietly as possible as Kate speaks to Pamela

Kate (*as child*) Are you not playing?
Pamela (*as child*) I don't know.
Kate (*as child*) Are you a shy person?

Pamela nods

Are you a very, very shy person?
Pamela (*as child*) Yes.
Kate (*as child*) What's your name?
Pamela (*as child*) Pamela.
Kate (*as child*) My name is Kate.
Pamela (*as child*) I know.
Kate (*as child*) How do you know?
Pamela (*as child*) Someone told me.
Kate (*as child*) Who told you?
Pamela (*as child*) I've forgotten?
Kate (*as child*) You've forgotten?
Pamela (*as child*) I think so.
Kate (*as child*) You're not only a very, very shy person. You're also a very, very stupid person, aren't you?

Pamela hangs her head

Well, aren't you? Aren't you stupid?
Pamela (*as child*) Yes.
Kate (*as child*) Do you like Crispin?
Pamela (*as child*) Yes.
Kate (*as child*) How much do you like him?
Pamela (*as child*) I don't know.
Kate (*as child*) Yes you do. Do you like him a little weeny bit? Do you like him lots and lots and lots? Or do you like him more than anything else in the whole wide world?

Pamela (*as child*) I don't know.

Kate (*as child*) Don't you know anything?

Pamela (*as child*) I don't know.

Kate (*as child*) What do you want to be when you grow up? (*Mimicking her*) "I don't know. I don't know."

Pamela (*as child*) Yes I do.

Kate (*as child*) What then?

Pamela (*as child*) I want to be like my mummy.

Kate (*as child*) What?

Pamela (*as child*) I want to be a housewife like my mummy. I want to have a home of my own. And a fridge. And a freezer. And a husband. And a washing-machine. And——

Kate (*as child*) You're too shy.

Pamela (*as child*) Pardon?

Kate (*as child*) You're too shy to have a husband. You're too shy to have anything. You're too shy to be alive, aren't you? Aren't you?

Pamela (*as child*) I don't know.

Kate (*as child*) You should be a bully. Bullies are lovely. Bullies get attention. Bullies are cruel. Bullies pull little girls' hair. (*She pulls Pamela's hair*) Bullies pinch little girls on the arm. (*She pinches Pamela on the arm*)

Pamela (*as child*) Don't. Leave me alone.

Kate (*as child*) Bullies never leave shy little girls alone. Bullies are nasty to shy little girls. Bullies are awful and horrible and hateful to shy little girls.

She is wrestling with Pamela now

Pamela breaks free, sobbing, and exits round the side of the house

Sheila (*as Julia, very loudly*) Catch it.

The ball hit by Graham is soaring into the air. Mrs Mitten puts her arms round the back of her neck and cowers. Ernest pushes her out of the way

Ernest (*as child*) Get out of my way. It's mine. I've got it. It's coming to me.

Sheila (*as Julia*) Mind the cat.

Ernest (*as child*) What?

Sheila (*as Julia*) I said——

With a scream Ernest falls headlong over the cat. Graham and Sheila burst out with laughter and then fall upon him. They have a real rough and tumble on the ground. Mrs Mitten cowers. Kate approaches and looks down on them with icy contempt

SCENE 9

The drawing-room. A few seconds later

Pamela is standing at the french windows bellowing at the invisible children still rough and tumbling on the lawn

Pamela That's quite enough of that, thank you very much. On your feet.

Let's have some discipline, if you please. Crispin—on your feet at once. Thank you. Now then, all of you, into the kitchen and wash those hands and knees.

One of the children complains

I don't care if it's a party. You still have to be neat and clean. Look at that little girl there. She's lovely and clean, isn't she? What's your name, dear?

Kate speaks

Kate. What a lovely name. There was a Kate used to live here, you know. She was ... (*She stares hard at the invisible Kate*) ... she was ... (*Briskly*) Yes, well, into the kitchen, wash and scrub and then we'll all go into the lounge and play games. Hide and seek. Sardines. Charades.

Crispin speaks

You might not want charades, Crispin. But that's not the point, is it? Our other little friends might want to play charades and hide and seek and sardines, mightn't they?

All the children shout out

Oh yes you do. You're going to have games. And you're going to enjoy them. Into that kitchen. Now. At once.

She exits through the french windows shooing them off

SCENE 10

The drawing-room. A few minutes later

The children are in the kitchen scrubbing themselves. Graham and Ernest are surreptitiously stuffing themselves with party goodies

Ernest I say, old boy. It's a damn fine blancmange, is this. Excellento.
Graham Well, don't spill any on your chin or Pamela'll know we've raided the buffet.
Ernest (*laughing*) Good wheeze, what? Raiding the buffet. Good wheeze. How many sausage rolls did you have?
Graham Three.
Ernest Three? Is that all?
Graham Yes. How many did you have?
Ernest Seventeen.
Graham You liar.
Ernest I'm not. I had seventeen sausage rolls, three gingerbread-men and half an individual trifle.
Graham It's all very strange isn't it? Very strange. Very spooky.
Ernest Beg pardon?
Graham Very, very strange. (*He begins to walk slowly round the room*) Hullo,

bookcase. Everything all right, chief? Not standing in a draught? Good, good. Stand easy. Keep up the good work.

Ernest continues to gobble up blancmange

Hullo, standard lamp. Any complaints? Got a good spot here, have you? Good, good. Glad to have you aboard. Carry on shining. (*He turns to Ernest*) It's all very, very strange. Ernest. That little girl.
Ernest Beautiful, old boy. Excellento.
Graham Yes. Yes.
Ernest Imagine her grown up.
Graham Yes. Yes.
Ernest Beautiful, eh?
Graham Yes. Beautiful. Ernest?
Ernest Yes, old boy?
Graham Were we like them when we were kids?
Ernest Oh yes, old boy. Ra-ther.

He falls very slowly off his chair as he did when he was a child. Graham laughs. Immediately the invisible children spring in from the kitchen. Both men cower

Graham All right, all right. All right, kids. Calm down. Cool it. (*He screams*) Shut up.

Pause

Thank you. Now perhaps somebody will tell me what's going on? Crispin? Julia?

Kate speaks

Thank you, Kate. Now then in your own time. Tell me what's going on.

Pamela enters

Pamela I'll tell you what's going on. We've all given our hands and knees a thorough scrubbing. And now we're going to play hide and seek.

Crispin speaks

Oh yes we are, Crispin. And after that we're going to play charades and——

Crispin speaks

I don't care whether your mother approves or not, Crispin. While you are under this roof you will obey my rules and you'll . . . Ernest.
Ernest Yes?
Pamela What is that pink stuff on your chin?
Ernest Pink stuff?
Pamela We've been at the blancmange, haven't we?
Ernest No.
Pamela Ernest!
Ernest Well, only a little bit.
Pamela Into the kitchen.

Ernest Beg pardon?
Pamela Into the kitchen. Wash that face. Scrub those hands. And wipe those
  sausage-roll crumbs off your cardigan.
Ernest Beg pardon?
Pamela Out. Out, out, out.
Ernest Can't I play hide and seek?
Pamela Out.

Ernest exits

Now then, children, are we all ready? I'll start you off. I'll seek and you can
hide.

Kate speaks

No, Kate, I don't think Mr Carey is going to play. You don't want to play,
do you, Graham?
Graham No.
Pamela Of course you don't.

Kate speaks

Well, you see, Kate, Mr Carey is a grown-up. And grown-ups don't——
Graham (*very gently*) Go and play, Kate. Go and hide away.

Pause. Pamela stares at him for a moment

Pamela (*clapping her hands briskly*) Right. Off you go. I'll close my eyes,
  count up to fifty and then I'll be on your trail. Off you go. (*She closes her
  eyes and begins to count*)

*Graham stands stock still staring at the door out of which Kate and the children
have rushed. Kate's voice is heard from outside while Pamela is still counting*

Kate (*off*) This way, little boy. Come with me. I know of a good place to hide
  away. No-one will ever find us there. Come on, little boy. I won't hurt you.
  I won't harm you. Come on, little boy. Come on.

*The Lights fade slowly with Graham staring hard at the door and Pamela still
counting*

SCENE 11

The drawing-room. A few minutes later

Ernest is hiding behind the door. Pamela's voice can be heard still counting, off

Pamela (*off*) Forty-six, forty-seven, forty-eight, forty-nine. Fifty. I'm
  coming. I'm on my way.

The door begins to open slowly

Ernest (*as child*) Who is it? Who's there?

The door opens more. Ernest cowers back

Who is it, who is it?

Pamela (as child) enters

Oh, it's you—old droopy-drawers.

Pamela (*as child*) I'm sorry. I'll find somewhere else to hide.

Ernest (*as child*) No. Don't.

Pamela (*as child*) Pardon?

Ernest (*as child*) You can stay here if you want. (*He pauses*) Droopy-drawers.

Pamela (*as child*) I haven't got droopy drawers.

Ernest (*as child*) Yes you have.

Pamela (*as child*) I haven't.

Ernest (*as child*) Show me then.

Pamela (*as child*) No.

Ernest (*as child*) Why not?

Pamela (*as child*) Because.

Ernest (*as child*) What's your name, droopy-drawers?

Pamela (*as child*) Pamela.

Ernest (*as child*) Pamela? That's a silly name. That's a soppy name.

Pamela (*as child*) So's Ernest.

Ernest (*as child*) I know. Do you like Barry Manilow?

Pamela (*as child*) Who's he?

Ernest (*as child*) Who's Barry Manilow? He's a singer, soppy. He's a singer, droopy-drawers. He's horrible. Just like you. He's a wet. Just like you. He's a drip. Just like you. I hate you and I'm going to pull your hair. (*He advances on her*)

Pamela (*as child, very softly*) You can pull my drawers down, if you like.

Ernest (*as child*) Beg pardon?

Pamela (*as child*) You can pull my drawers down.

Ernest (*as child*) I say. Really?

Pamela (*as child*) Yes.

Ernest (*as child*) Really, really, really?

Pamela (*as child*) Really, really, really.

Ernest (*as child*) I say. Excellento.

Pause. He looks thoroughly uncomfortable

Yes. I say.

Pamela (*as child*) Don't you know what to do?

Ernest (*as child*) Beg pardon?

Pamela (*as child*) Don't you know what to do?

Ernest (*as child*) Who? Me? Course I know what to do. What do you mean—don't I know what to do? Course I know what to do.

Pamela (*as child*) Well do it.

Ernest (*as child*) Beg pardon?

Pamela (*as child*) Kiss me. Come on, kiss me.

He is very embarrassed. She moves towards him nervously. They both pucker their lips and begin to lean in towards each other clumsily

  Mrs Mitten (as a child) enters

Ernest (*as child*) What do you want?
Mrs Mitten (*as child*) I'm hiding.
Ernest (*as child*) Not here you're not.
Mrs Mitten (*as child*) Yes I am.
Ernest (*as child*) No you're not.
Mrs Mitten (*as child*) You can't stop me.
Ernest (*as child*) I can. I'll pull your drawers down just like I've done hers. (*He advances on her*)
Mrs Mitten (*as child, screaming*) Ah. Telling on you. Telling.

  Mrs Mitten exits

Black-out

Pamela (*during the Black-out*) Got you. The fat little boy in the drawing-room. And the shy little girl standing next to him. Got you. Right then, everyone else. I'm coming. I'm on your trail.

SCENE 12

The bedroom. A few minutes later

Kate as a child and Graham as Crispin are looking at each other

Mrs Mitten (as a child) bursts in

Graham and Kate turn to her savagely

Kate
Graham } (*together*) Get out!

  Mrs Mitten turns instantly and exits

Kate (*as child*) Isn't she awful?
Graham (*as Crispin*) Yes.
Kate (*as child*) Do you like her?
Graham (*as Crispin*) No.
Kate (*as child*) Neither do I. Do you like this room?
Graham (*as Crispin*) I don't know.
Kate (*as child*) I do. I think this is a very loving room. Do you know what I mean, little boy?
Graham (*as Crispin*) Don't call me "little boy".
Kate (*as child*) Do you like your name?
Graham (*as Crispin*) No.
Kate (*as child*) Would you rather be called something else?
Graham (*as Crispin*) I don't know.

Kate (*as child*) Yes you do. If you weren't called Crispin, what would you rather be called?

Graham (*as Crispin*) Er ... er ...

Kate (*as child*) Graham.

Graham (*as Crispin*) What?

Kate (*as child*) Graham. Would you like to be called Graham?

Graham (*as Crispin, after a pause*) Yes.

Kate (*as child*) When you grow up, would you like to marry me?

Graham (*as Crispin*) I don't know.

Kate (*as child*) Would you like me to live with you in this house? You and I, little boy. All alone in this house. And we'd have lots of babies and a Newfoundland dog. Would you like that?

Graham (*as Crispin*) Yes. I've always wanted to have a Newfoundland dog.

Kate (*as child*) And why have you always wanted me to live with you?

Graham (*as Crispin*) I don't know.

Kate (*as child*) Why, little boy? Why?

Graham (*as Crispin*) Because I think you're beautiful.

Kate (*as child*) Say it again.

Graham (*as Crispin*) I think you're beautiful.

Kate (*as child*) Say it again.

Graham (*as Crispin*) Don't want to.

Kate (*as child*) Say it again, little boy.

Graham (*as Crispin*) I think you're beautiful.

Kate (*as child*) You can kiss me if you want.

Graham (*as Crispin*) I don't know how to.

Kate (*as child*) I'll show you. Come here, little boy. Come to me. I won't hurt you.

He moves towards her. She takes him in her arms and kisses him long and hard. Slowly she forces him back on to the bed

Mrs Mitten enters

Mrs Mitten (*as child*) Ah. Ah, I'm telling on you. I'm telling the grown-ups.

Mrs Mitten exits

Black-out

Pamela (*during the Black-out*) Where are you then? Where are you all? I'm after you. I'm hot on the trail. You'll never get away.

Scene 13

The drawing-room. A few minutes later

Ernest as a child and Sheila as Julia are in a deep and long embrace

Mrs Mitten enters from the hall

Mrs Mitten (*as child*) Ah. Ah, I'm telling on you. I'm telling the grown-ups.

She races across the room and exits through the french windows

Ernest kisses Sheila again

Sheila (*as Julia, pushing him away*) Why did you do that?
Ernest (*as child*) What?
Sheila (*as Julia*) Kiss me.
Ernest (*as child*) Because you look like my school dentist.
Sheila (*as Julia*) What?
Ernest (*as child*) She's very nice. She rides an auto-cycle. With a crash helmet. And gauntlets. And she's very beautiful, too.
Sheila (*as Julia*) Am I beautiful, too?
Ernest (*as child*) Ra-ther. Excellento.
Sheila (*as Julia*) When you grow up, would you like to marry me?
Ernest (*as child*) Ra-ther.
Sheila (*as Julia*) No you wouldn't.
Ernest (*as child*) Beg pardon?
Sheila (*as Julia*) You'd rather marry droopy-drawers.
Ernest (*as child*) No I wouldn't.
Sheila (*as Julia*) Honestly?
Ernest (*as child*) Honestly. I'd marry you.
Sheila (*as Julia*) Why?
Ernest (*as child*) Beg pardon?
Sheila (*as Julia*) Why would you marry me?
Ernest (*as child*) Because ... because ... because you can play tunes on privet leaves.
Sheila (*as Julia*) Can you?
Ernest (*as child*) No.
Sheila (*as Julia*) Would you like me to teach you?
Ernest (*as child*) Ra-ther.
Sheila (*as Julia*) Or would you like me to teach you how to kiss heaps and heaps and heaps better than you do now?
Ernest (*as child*) Beg pardon?
Sheila (*as Julia*) Come here. I'm going to show you how grown-ups kiss in those plays on telly. (*She approaches him and embraces him*)

Pamela shouts from outside. They freeze

Pamela (*off*) I know you're in there. I'm coming to get you. You're caught.
Sheila (*as Julia*) Quick. The garden.

She drags Ernest by the hand through the french windows

Pamela enters immediately from the hall

Pamela Got you. You're ... (*She looks around*) Ah. You're hiding, are you? Well, I know you're in here. I saw you come in. You can't get away from me. And you, little fat boy. You've already been caught. You're a nasty cheat. And you deserve a good smack bottie. (*She begins to search*) No use hiding. Pamela's caught you. I know your little game. I've known it all along. When we're found out, we give up, don't we? Come on. Give yourselves up. You're caught. (*She pauses, notices the open french windows, dashes to them and shouts out*) I can see you. Behind the rain butt. No. Don't run away. You're caught. Back to the lounge and wait for the others. Off you go. Chop, chop, chop.

Graham enters from the hall

Graham Have you seen Ernest?
Pamela (*turning*) No.
Graham I expect he's hiding.
Pamela Hiding?
Graham From the kids.
Pamela (*laughing*) Poor Ernest.
Graham There are kids everywhere. I just went into my bedroom and caught a couple of them snogging on the bed.
Pamela They were what?
Graham Snogging.
Pamela And what did you do?
Graham Coughed rather loudly. And left them to it.
Pamela You left them to it?
Graham There's no harm in it, Pamela. They're only children.
Pamela Only children? Do you realize what children are like these days, Graham? They're not like us when we were children. They're so mature these days. Mentally mature. Physically mature. Good gracious me, Graham, there are Olympic swimming champions just stepped out of their cradles. And what about those awful ice skaters with their spotty faces?
Graham Don't worry, Pamela. They're all right. They're only children. Relax. Take it easy. If you want to worry about something, worry about us. We're adults. We need much more worrying about than the children.

Pause

Is there any of that sherry left?
Pamela I wonder how you and I would have reacted to each other if we'd met as children.
Graham Sorry?
Pamela At a party, say. How would we have behaved?
Graham You'd have bullied me to death.
Pamela I've told you. I was very shy when I was a little girl. I never said a word. I used to stand in a corner. And no-one ever wanted to kiss me.
Graham Poor old you.
Pamela Once I plucked up courage and asked a boy to kiss me.
Graham And what happened?
Pamela Nothing. He didn't know how to.
Graham I did.
Pamela I bet you did.
Graham I was very good at it. I was brill.
Pamela Would you have kissed me?
Graham Oh yes. I kissed everybody.
Pamela So I wouldn't have been special?

Pause. Graham looks at her intently

Graham Do you know, Pamela, I rather think you might have been.

Pamela Do you, Graham?

Graham Yes. I think . . . no, I'm certain that if we'd met at a party, I'd have kissed you. A really special kiss. Really, really special. A long, slow, lingering kiss. A tender kiss. A passionate kiss.

Pamela Show me.

Graham What?

Pamela Show me. Now.

She walks to him very slowly. They are about to embrace

At that moment, Ernest enters through the french windows

Ernest I want to go home.

Pamela What?

Ernest I want to go home. I'm bored.

Pamela Nonsense.

Ernest It's not nonsense. I'm bored. And I've got toothache, too. By jingo, I could just do with a swift appointment with my dentist.

Pamela Ernest!

Ernest Yes?

Pamela You're bumbling again.

Ernest I know. I was bumbling out there in the garden. I was bumbling so much I could have sworn I saw Kate.

Graham Kate?

Ernest Yes.

Pamela Ernest, you're being silly again.

Ernest No I'm not. I was standing by the greenhouse. And I saw this white car. An MG.

Graham Kate's got a white MG.

Ernest I know. And the girl who was driving it was wearing a red jacket. Like a hunting jacket. With a hood. And sort of furry things on it.

Graham Kate's got a jacket like that. It must have been Kate. So what happened next?

Ernest Well, the car drove up the road very slowly. And . . . and . . .

Graham And what, Ernest?

Ernest Well, I blinked, old boy. And when I looked again, it had gone.

Graham It had gone? What do you mean, it had gone?

Ernest It always happens when I'm bumbling. I see things very clearly, and then I blink, and they disappear.

Graham I don't follow you, Ernest.

Ernest Nobody ever does. I'm that sort of person.

Pamela I think we should drop the subject, don't you, Graham?

Graham No, I don't. What are you getting at, Ernest? You say you saw Kate. And then you say she disappeared. What's going on?

Ernest It's me bumbling, old boy. I'm always doing it. I'm sitting in a room, standing in a pub, having a bath, shampooing the dog—that sort of rot— and then someone appears in front of me. Very clearly. Very precisely. I can see them as clearly as I can see you two now. When I was doing my ablutions the other day I saw Lord Baden-Powell. He was eating a fig. And then yesterday when I was sitting in the garden throwing stones at the cat, I saw Dwight D. Eisenhower. He was eating a fig, too. And, do you know, only a few minutes ago I was sitting here in the drawing-room, and I saw as clear as anything the first girl I ever kissed.

Pamela I see. We're getting to "that time of life", are we? Our old sweethearts are cropping up now, are they, Ernest?

Ernest She wasn't an old sweetheart. She was just a girl I kissed. At a party. She was rather pretty. And I kissed her. And I saw her again. Right here.

Graham Never mind the girl at the party. What about Kate?

Ernest Same as the girl at the party, old boy. Disappeared. It was just me. Bumbling away. As usual.

Graham Yes, but it might have been Kate.

Pamela I can assure you it wasn't, Graham. It was just Ernest and his bumbling.

Graham's shoulders crumble

You've got to reconcile yourself to it. Kate is not going to come back.

Graham (*weakly*) I know.

Pamela Kate is finished. Banish her from your mind.

Graham I loved her.

Pamela I know.

Graham This house is bursting at the seams. Yet without her it's empty. She used to pad round the house with nothing on.

Ernest Really, old boy? I love seeing women with no togs on.

Pamela (*hissing*) Ernest!

Ernest Sorry.

Graham And she'd creep into my workroom. I wouldn't hear. I'd be concentrating on a model. And she'd just touch the back of my neck with her breath. And it wouldn't make me jump. It was as though she'd been there all the time and I'd grown used to her presence, so I wasn't surprised when she breathed on my neck, and I'd turn to her, and I'd smile, and she'd take me by the hand, and she'd say: "Come on, little boy. Come with me. I won't hurt you." I'm so lonely. I want Kate. I'm lonely.

Ernest and Pamela move slowly towards him

Ernest (*diffidently putting his arm round Graham*) So am I, old boy.

Pamela (*putting her arms round both of them*) We all are, Graham. We're all desperately lonely. All grown-ups are.

They hug each other. The invisible Crispin enters from the hall. He speaks. They all turn to him

Graham Don't do that, Crispin. Knock before you come in. How many more times have I to tell you to——

Pamela What do you want, Crispin?

Crispin speaks

A play, Crispin? What sort of play are you going to do?

Crispin speaks

Graham A play about us?
Pamela How nice. How charming, Crispin. What a lovely idea. Isn't it a lovely idea, Daddy?
Graham I don't know. I suspect there's a minefield there, Pamela.
Pamela Nonsense, Graham. It's perfectly sweet of them, and I'm sure we'll all be enchanted. And what are you going to call the play, Crispin?

Crispin speaks

You Should See Us Now? I see. Well, it's a novel sort of title and——

Crispin speaks

Yes, we're ready. We're all ready, aren't we, Daddy?
Graham (*gloomily*) Oh yes, we're ready.

Crispin speaks

Pamela Yes, Crispin. You go back and get your . . . fellow Thespians. And come in just as soon as you like.

Crispin speaks

Yes, yes. We're really looking forward to it. Now off you pop and we'll get everything ready.

Crispin exits

Ernest Oh Lord, I hate this sort of thing. Can't we go home, Pamela?
Graham You're not going home now, matey. This is my hour of need. You can't desert me now.
Pamela There's no question of desertion, Graham. Ernest.
Ernest Yes, old boy?
Pamela Pull yourself together.
Ernest Yes, old boy.
Pamela Now then, let's get everything arranged. Ernest, chairs. Put them in a line. Come on. Chop, chop, chop. Do you know, Graham, I'm really looking forward to this. How sweet of them. How charming.

Ernest arranges the chairs in a line. They all sit down facing the door

(*Shouting*) Ready. We're ready, children.

Immediately Sheila and Mrs Mitten enter from the french windows

Sheila So? So this is how we find you, is it?
Graham Sheila.
Sheila What is this then? The Grand Inquisition? Looking for another poor innocent child to torture, are we?
Pamela What are you doing here?
Mrs Mitten You might well ask.
Pamela I do. And I repeat. What are you doing here?

Mrs Mitten We've come to deal with you.

Pamela Me?

Mrs Mitten Yes, you.

Sheila Mother, let me deal with this.

Mrs Mitten No I will not. As I say, I'm their grandmother just as much as what you are and I'm going to have my say.

Graham What say?

Mrs Mitten My say about her.

Ernest What about her, for Pete's sake? Stop bumbling, woman. Can't stand bumbling in other people.

Mrs Mitten Oh you can't stand it, can't you? Mr Lah-di-dah can't stand it. Well, I can't stand what your wife has been doing to my grandchildren.

Pamela What?

Mrs Mitten Don't come that innocent look with me. Child-batterer!

Graham Child-batterer? What the hell are you talking about?

Mrs Mitten I'm talking about her beating the living daylights out of my grandchildren. I'm talking about——

Graham Wait a minute. Now calm down. Cool it.

Pause

Sheila. What is your mother talking about?

Sheila She's talking about our children, Graham. She's talking about the telephone call Crispin made to me this afternoon.

Graham What telephone call?

Sheila He was distraught. Absolutely beside himself.

Graham About what?

Mrs Mitten About her beating the living daylights out of Crispin and Julia.

Ernest I say. Steady on.

Sheila Never mind "Steady on", Ernest. This is a very, very serious matter.

Mrs Mitten She wants locking up, that's what she wants. I told you we should never have left them.

Sheila Mother! Will you kindly shut up.

Mrs Mitten Oooh, she tells her own mother to shut up. There. See what you've done now, child-batterer. You've made my daughter turn on her own mother.

Graham Shut up. Shut up, you old bat. Now then, Sheila, what precisely did Crispin tell you?

Sheila He told me that Pamela had been using physical force on them. He told me she's hit him with a rolling-pin. He told me she's pulled Julia's hair, twisted her arm and tried to pull her knickers down.

Pamela I never.

Sheila He told me that ever since they had entered this house they'd been subjected to a constant regime of bullying by her.

Pamela I'm not a bully.

Mrs Mitten You are.

Pamela I'm not.

Mrs Mitten You are.

Pamela I'm not a bully, am I, Ernest? I'm shy, I am. I'm very, very, very shy.

Mrs Mitten Fibber. Typical, is that. Get bullies into a corner and what do they do—start the tears and the bellyaching and they try to lie their way out of things. As I say, I was brought up in a hard school and——

Graham If I hear you say that once again, I'll——

Sheila You'll what?

Graham I'll . . . I'll . . . I'll grab hold of her by the hair and I'll . . . I'll . . . I'll pull her knickers down.

Mrs Mitten Ah. Telling on you.

Ernest Don't care, don't care. Come on, everyone. Let's chase her and pull her knickers down.

Mrs Mitten (*beginning to scream*) Ah. Ah, I'm telling on you. I'm telling.

Ernest, Graham and Pamela advance on Mrs Mitten

Sheila Just you leave her alone.

Graham "Just you leave her alone." Yar yar yer yar yar. We're going to pull her knickers down.

Mrs Mitten Get off me. Leave me alone.

They begin to pile into each other

    Kate enters through the french windows. She is wearing the red jacket described by Ernest. She looks at them for a moment

Kate Stop it. Stop it this instant.

They stop. They turn to her

    Kids. How I hate kids.

Graham Kate! Kate, you've come back.

Kate Yes, I've come back.

Graham Oh, Kate. Kate, Kate, Kate.

Kate (*taking him by the hand*) Come with me, little boy. I won't harm you. I won't hurt you. Come with me. I love you, little boy. I love you heaps and heaps and heaps.

    Kate leads him by the hand out of the french windows

Silence

Pamela Now what do we do?

Ernest Only one thing for it, old girl. (*He climbs on a chair and very, very slowly falls off it*)

Black-out

CURTAIN

FURNITURE AND PROPERTY LIST

ACT I

SCENE 1. *The Drawing-room*

On stage: Table
Chair
2 armchairs. *On them:* cushions
Dresser. *On it:* table lamp

Off stage: Tray with bottle of wine and glass **(Graham)**

Personal: **Graham:** wrist-watch (required throughout)

SCENE 2. *The Garden*

On stage: Shrubs
Bushes, including privet bush with leaves

Off stage: Bottle of wine, glass **(Graham)**

SCENE 3. *The Drawing-room*

On stage: As Scene 1
Set: Pocket compass on table

Off stage: Facecloth **(Mrs Mitten)**

SCENE 4. *The Garden*

On stage: As Scene 2

Set: Cricket bat (for **Pamela**)

SCENE 5. *The Drawing-room*

On stage: As Scene 1

SCENE 6. *The Children's Bedroom*

On stage: Double bed with bedding. *Above it:* light
Fireplace
Window curtains (*closed*)

SCENE 7.   *The Drawing-room*
On stage: As Scene 1

ACT II

SCENE 1.   *The Garden*
On stage: As Act I, Scene 2

SCENE 2.   *The Drawing-room*
On stage: As Act I, Scene 1

Set: Newspaper (for **Ernest)**

Off stage: Privet leaf **(Graham)**
             Dirty sock **(Pamela)**

SCENE 3.   *The Children's Bedroom*
On stage: As Act I, Scene 6

Set: **Sheila**'s dress on bed

SCENE 4.   *The Drawing-room*
On stage: As Act I, Scene 1

Off stage: Telephone **(Graham)**
             Tray with bottle of sherry and 3 glasses **(Pamela)**

SCENE 5.   *The Drawing-room*
On stage: Sofa
             2 armchairs
             Bookcase. *In it:* books
             Standard lamp
             Sideboard

SCENE 6.   *The Drawing-room*
On stage: As Act I, Scene 1

Check: Glasses of sherry for **Pamela**, **Ernest** and **Graham**

SCENE 7.   *The Drawing-room*
On stage: As Act II, Scene 5

SCENE 8.   *The Garden*
On stage: As Act I, Scene 2

Set: Cricket bat (for **Mrs Mitten)**

SCENE 9.   *The Drawing-room*
On stage: As Act I, Scene 1

SCENE 10.   *The Drawing-room*
On stage: As Act II, Scene 5

Set: Party food on sideboard

SCENE 11.   *The Drawing-room*
On stage: As Act I, Scene 1

SCENE 12.   *The Bedroom*
On stage: As Act I, Scene 6

SCENE 13.   *The Drawing-room*
On stage: As Act I, Scene 1

LIGHTING PLOT

Practical fittings required: table lamp, standard lamp, light above bed
Various interior and exterior settings: a drawing-room, a garden, a bedroom, a lounge

ACT I, Scene 1.   Afternoon

To open: General interior lighting
No cues

ACT I, Scene 2.   Afternoon

To open: General exterior lighting
No cues

ACT I, Scene 3.   Afternoon

To open: General interior lighting

Cue 1	**Graham:** "... prize delphiniums." *Black-out*	(Page 19)

ACT I, Scene 4.   Evening

To open: General exterior lighting
No cues

ACT I, Scene 5.   Evening

To open: General interior lighting, table lamp on

Cue 2	**Graham:** "Kate. Oh, Kate." *Slowly fade to Black-out*	(Page 26)

ACT I, Scene 6.   Evening

To open: Children's bedroom in darkness; light on landing

Cue 3	**Pamela** and **Ernest** exit *Snap off landing light*	(Page 27)
Cue 4	**Graham** (*as Crispin*): "Great." (*He switches on the light above the bed*) *Snap on light above bed and covering spot*	(Page 27)
Cue 5	**Sheila** (*as Julia*): "Right. I will." (*She switches off the light*) *Snap off light above bed and covering spot; snap on light as* **Graham** *switches it on; snap off as* **Sheila** *switches it off; snap on as* **Graham** *switches it on*	(Page 27)

Cue 6   **Sheila** switches off light   (Page 28)
           Snap off light and covering spot; snap on again as **Graham**
               switches it on

Cue 7   **Sheila** switches off light   (Page 28)
           Snap off light and covering spot; then snap on again as **Graham**
               switches it on

Cue 8   **Sheila** switches off light   (Page 30)
           Snap off light and covering spot

ACT I, Scene 7.   Evening

To open: General interior lighting, table lamp on

Cue 9   **Sheila** (*as Julia*): "... to go home. Now."   (Page 32)
           Black-out

ACT II, Scene 1.   Mid-morning

To open: General exterior lighting

No cues

ACT II, Scene 2.   Mid-morning

To open: General interior lighting

No cues

ACT II, Scene 3.   Afternoon

To open: General interior lighting

No cues

ACT II, Scene 4.   Afternoon

To open: General interior lighting

No cues

ACT II, Scene 5.   Afternoon

To open: General interior lighting

No cues

ACT II, Scene 6.   Afternoon

To open: General interior lighting

Cue 10   **Graham:** "Your name is Kate?"   (Page 47)
           Black-out

ACT II, Scene 7.   Afternoon

To open: General interior lighting

Cue 11   **Kate:** "... go out and play cricket?"   (Page 49)
           Slowly fade to Black-out

ACT II, SCENE 8.   Afternoon

To open: General exterior lighting

No cues

ACT II, SCENE 9.   Afternoon

To open: General interior lighting

No cues

ACT II, SCENE 10.   Afternoon

To open   General interior lighting

Cue 12   **Kate:** ". . . little boy. Come on."   (Page 54)
             Slowly fade to Black-out

ACT II, SCENE 11.   Afternoon

To open: General interior lighting

Cue 13   **Mrs Mitten** exits   (Page 56)
             Black-out

ACT II, SCENE 12.   Afternoon

To open: General interior lighting

Cue 14   **Mrs Mitten** exits   (Page 57)
             Black-out

ACT II, SCENE 13.   Afternoon

To open: General interior lighting

Cue 15   **Ernest** falls off the chair   (Page 64)
             Black-out

EFFECTS PLOT

ACT I

Cue 1   **Pamela:** "... about to deal with you."   (Page 30)
Footsteps on stairs

ACT II

Cue 2   **Graham:** "... next five hours."   (Page 40)
Telephone rings